The Romance of Teaching

The Romance of Teaching

Montessori in the Elementary School

Ann V. Angell

Published by Wheatmark®
1760 East River Road, Suite 145
Tucson, Arizona 85718 USA
www.wheatmark.com

Includes bibliographical references. 1. Montessori method of education. 2. Education, elementary.

ISBN: 978-1-62787-152-5 (paperback)
ISBN: 978-1-62787-153-2 (ebook)
LCCN: 2014947330

For Scott, Sabine, Kofi, and Kai

Contents

Acknowledgements

Success as a teacher depends on the support and contributions of many people. I am deeply grateful for the administrators who hired me, the community of teachers who inspired me, the parents who always said yes, and the children who often said no because they had a better idea. They are still my best friends.

I don't know of a job closer to herding cats than being a Montessori administrator. I have had the good fortune to work with the very best, people who trusted my judgment, provided the resources I needed, and nurtured me so that I could nurture the children in my classrooms. Dr. Martha Urioste's vision and commitment to Montessori in a public school gave me an opportunity I could hardly have imagined when I began my career. Later she encouraged me to write this book. Joe Seidel, Sharon Dubble, Beth Samples, Karin Salzmann, and Jesse Berchenko were all gifted leaders who brought families and teachers together to create dynamic learning opportunities for children in private Montessori schools. It was a privilege to work for each of them.

Most of my best ideas, many shared in this book, have come from observing other teachers and, in some lucky cases, teaching with them. Nikki Torres, Kathy Kelley,

Charleen Seidel, and Phil Gang were all wonderful co-teachers who shared their ideas and supported mine. I learned much from observing classrooms guided by Tim Nee, Betty Litsey, and Kate Ramsey. Iris Fogarrasey taught me about A-Cute Turkeys and how to challenge individual students to do their best. Christy Berger was the best assistant ever and continued to inspire me when she began teaching her own class. There were always teachers around me with more experience willing to help me solve problems, and there were always younger teachers around me with new ideas and loads of enthusiasm. I wish I could thank them all personally.

I could not have succeeded in my profession without the dedicated support of parents. They attended meetings, accompanied me on camping trips, bought books for the class, and drove students all over town to enrich their learning experiences. One parent, Matt Kirsch, read the first draft of this book and then asked the right questions to guide a major revision.

Friends Paula Hill and Carolyn MacAdam both took time to read the revised draft and made excellent suggestions. Montessori teachers Tina Barath and Mandi Prout also read chapters and assured me teachers would find validation in my story.

Finally, the team at Wheatmark, including Grael Norton, Lori Leavitt, and Atilla Vekony, guided this project across the finish line. I thank all of these people for their encouragement and assistance.

Ann V. Angell

Introduction

As confidence in traditional schooling continues to shrink, interest in Montessori education is expanding rapidly in the United States. More than five hundred public schools in forty-two states offer Montessori for elementary students, and some have upper-level programs as well. Many of the thousands of Montessori preschools have also added elementary classes because parents insist. Why should joyful learning cease after kindergarten? They know the early habits of learning predict adult well-being.

In fact, many who walk tall among us credit Montessori with their success. Google founders, Larry Page and Sergey Brin, say they were encouraged to pursue their own interests and became self-directed in Montessori schools. Jeff Bezos, who started Amazon, attributes his confidence to the nurturing environment of Montessori classes, which he attended through grade three. Wikipedia founder Jimmy Wales associates Montessori with becoming a keen reader and intellectually curious. Culinary genius Julia Childs learned to love working with her hands. Author Gabriel Garcia Marquez became sensitive to beauty and curious about the secrets of life. Video game pioneer Will Wright experienced the joy of discovery.

Montessori gave me the love of teaching.

I had begun to question whether education was a good fit for me after two years teaching high school English. Then, while trying to find the right preschool for my toddler, I visited a Montessori class. In a quiet, orderly environment, I watched three-year-olds slicing apples with care and tracing sandpaper letters with their fingertips. Older children were writing and computing large sums. Every child seemed to act independently with purpose and dignity. I could hardly find the teachers. Like many other parents who have described amazement upon first observing a Montessori preschool class, I became an instant convert.

Soon after that observation, I enrolled my son, Scott, in the primary class at a suburban Montessori school in Stamford, Connecticut. When he turned six, he joined their elementary class. It was a noisier place where students were often working in small groups and interacting more with adults, but the same intellectual fervor seemed to prevail. What I saw was another way to learn and a better way to teach.

I became acquainted with Scott's teachers, two young men who had recently completed the training course at the Center for International Montessori Studies in Bergamo, Italy. It was the only place in the world preparing Montessori elementary teachers in the early 1970s. They assured me the course was both a grand adventure and a transformative education.

And so with a supportive husband and a seven-year-old eager to see the world, Scott and I went to Italy for a year. We spent the first two months in Perugia. I studied Italian at the Universita per Stranieri. Scott set up a trading post on a narrow staircase near our apartment, selling candy by the piece and baseball cards from the United States. Not surprisingly, he learned Italian more quickly than I did in class.

In the late summer we moved north to the city of Bergamo, where I attended the Montessori course presented by Eleanor Honegger Caprotti and Camillo Grazzini. They delivered lectures in Italian, which were translated sentence by sentence into English. With a modest grasp of Italian, I understood both, making it possible to transcribe the lectures almost verbatim. Each night I typed up my notes using a black and red ribbon, reserving the red for exact phrases teachers would use during lessons. Years later, when I opened my album during a geometry seminar, someone exclaimed, "That looks like the Bible." Indeed, the Bergamo lessons guided my teaching, almost religiously, over the next thirty years.

In addition to attending the daily lectures, I observed classes at the local Montessori school in Bergamo, spent hours practicing with Montessori materials, and handcrafted about a hundred fraction and geometry charts. Taken together, the course of study did truly transform my ideas about teaching and learning.

When I returned to the States, my first job was starting an elementary class at the Montessori School of Woodstock, New York. It was challenging, but the director of the school and terrific parents supported all my experimental efforts. In subsequent years, I taught both lower and upper elementary classes at private Montessori schools in Atlanta, Georgia, and Wilton, Connecticut. I concluded my career teaching for a decade at a Montessori magnet school in the Denver Public Schools system.

Along the way I studied at Emory University, earning a masters and later a PhD in education. During that time I participated in cross-national studies of education, which took me to Japan for two years. I was inspired by John Dewey's ideas about democratic education and intrigued by emerging constructivist theory. Both seemed highly consistent with Dr. Montessori's theory of human development. Throughout my graduate studies, however, her work was never part of the conversation. When I wrote papers based on her ideas, professors and fellow students alike were keenly interested and often surprised. (See appendix A.)

Maria Montessori's contributions to our understanding of how children develop and learn are still absent from most academic programs purporting to prepare teachers. The reason may be that her cross-disciplinary thinking contradicts the traditionally separate domains in higher education. She was a medical doctor (the first woman MD in Italy), a psychologist, a theoretical thinker, an innovative designer of didactic material, and a deeply religious person. Throughout her long career, she integrated those commitments, moving smoothly and constantly between theory and practice. Edward O. Wilson's theory of consilience comes to mind. He asserts that answers to our future lie in the promise of unexpected insight and sound judgment made possible when disciplinary boundaries disappear. Montessori theory realized in a new kind of schooling exemplifies such an overlapping unity.

The year before I planned to retire from the magnet school where I had been teaching an upper elementary class, an unexpected number of second and third graders enrolled, creating the need for a "middle elementary class." I volunteered to be the teacher. Starting a new class is a challenge every time, and the unusual age-grouping required new thinking. Adjustments in the environment needed to be made and broader curricular opportunities planned. As the year progressed, there were frequent surprises, surges of intense interest, unexpected difficulties, and joyful celebrations. Over the space of nine months, I became increasingly enamored as I watched a caring community of engaged learners evolve.

My memory bank was overflowing when the school year ended, and retirement gave me time to reflect. I began to sift through my records of lessons and anecdotal notes. I stumbled on some poems students had written describing what they had learned. I began to write stories to capture what seemed more and more like an enchanted year. I borrowed the portfolio of one of the youngest boys in the class. His faithful journaling and carefully chosen work samples assured me I was not writing fairy tales.

Nevertheless, I wondered if it had been a truly unusual class in an extraordinary year. Probably not. In fact, I think it was an ordinary class in a typical year. The students were mixed by race, economic circumstance, academic capability, and background. There were only a few African American children, a population shrinking in our school. More than a third of the children were Hispanic, several from families who spoke no English at home. Five in the class were considered special-needs students with a variety of learning disabilities. Two fourth-grade girls had no previous experience in a Montessori class.

Adaptations to public school culture had to be made, sometimes in conflict with Montessori principles. A strong teachers' union required breaks for teacher planning time, so weekly art and music and library lessons compromised extended work periods. It was a year when the district mandated a new reading assessment for every student three times during the year, a paperwork nightmare and a time-consuming process. State tests for all levels consumed the entire month of March. It was the year of the Arab Spring. As with every class, many of the events that took place were unexpected, but most days were ordinary.

The time I had to reflect on the year's events was the extraordinary part. As I began to organize my stories, I recognized an array of teaching roles I had enacted. In her extensive writing about education, Dr. Montessori seldom used the word *teacher*, preferring designations for the adult such as *guide*, *companion*, or *scientist*. Rethinking the teacher's role changes the human dynamic in the classroom, not only transforming what the adult does, but also how students respond.

Before the students arrived, I thought of myself as a mapmaker preparing the classroom for exploration. When the school year began, I became a storyteller to inspire imaginations and stimulate interests. Soon I was able to enjoy the role of companion, accompanying individuals as they pursued self-directed pathways of learning. When the social order of the classroom began to break down, I became a community organizer; and by semester's end, I was acting as a mirror to reflect back to the students their unique talents and accomplishments.

Many of the children faced new personal obstacles in January, so I returned to the fundamental role of scientific observer, psychologizing the curriculum to meet special needs. When circumstances restricted excursions beyond the classroom, I became an in-house tour guide. In the testing month, I was an advocate for the students, and by April, I needed the enthusiasm of a ringmaster to revive the Montessori curriculum. As the school year concluded, I became the student, the learner.

Then came June and a wealth of time to be a reflective practitioner.

Teachers have so little time to reflect as they struggle to meet student needs, parents' expectations, and system demands. Montessori teaching is always experimental, replete with successes and failures, some efforts thwarted and others rewarded. Perhaps veteran teachers will find their own efforts validated here.

I hope these stories will also inspire teachers just entering the field. With the rapid expansion of Montessori schools, demand for trained teachers is increasing faster than the supply. Many will receive the briefest introduction to Montessori pedagogy without opportunities to practice teaching or observe practicing teachers. Perhaps this book will provide insight into the challenges they encounter starting new classes.

There are, of course, teachers everywhere who have experienced the romance of teaching. Perhaps they will find a kindred spirit on these pages.

Finally, if parents have visited a Montessori elementary classroom and wondered what in the world was going on in there, I hope this book will help them fall in love too.

The
Romance of
Teaching

1 August
The Mapmaker

We have learnt that child-psychology is not that of the adult, and its essential condition is freedom to act in a prepared environment where the child can be intelligently active.

—Maria Montessori[1]

Nothing engages a Montessori teacher more completely than preparing the learning environment. If you are setting up a new classroom, it can take the whole summer. For a week in August, I had been reviving the familiar space where I taught an upper elementary class. My work was interrupted when a special faculty meeting was called. The principal described an unusual bulge in the fall enrollment—too many second and third graders. She suggested the problem could be solved by creating a new middle elementary class.

In a moment of unguarded enthusiasm, I volunteered to be the teacher.

The fifth and sixth graders I was expecting were assigned to other classes. I knew I would miss their help as role models and leaders, but the prospect of starting the new class was intriguing. There would be fourth graders ready for advanced lessons and younger children eager for great stories and hands-on activities. It was an invitation to teach across the entire elementary Montessori curriculum, with forty-eight hours to rethink the classroom landscape. What adjustments would help a new group of students start down the path to self-directed learning?

Maria Montessori described students as active and intelligent explorers.[2] John Dewey characterized the process of education as a journey the child takes with help from a map, which is the curriculum. From both perspectives, every student must find a unique path and make the trip. (See appendix B.)

The Montessori teacher puts the map in the children's hands by preparing an environment to explore. Main routes suggest excursions into language, mathematics, geography, history, and science. There are points of interest, mountains to climb, landmarks, and places to rest. A river of art, music, dance, and drama meanders across the map's terrain. Arrows around the periphery suggest destinations beyond the classroom—libraries, museums, and community enterprises of all kinds where students might pursue their interests.

To encourage my young explorers, I made sure there were colorful hands-on materials on every shelf. Math shelves already held an enticing array of Montessori materials—bead frames, fraction insets, checkerboards for multiplying, and the racks and tubes for division. There was a showy display of blue geometric solids and the cabinet of plane figures on the geometry shelf to invite tracing, measuring, and design. (See appendices C and D.)

On the language shelves students would find a rainbow

parade of grammar boxes to explore the function of words—
black boxes for nouns, red for verbs, blue for adjectives,
and purple for prepositions. Older students sometimes said
the grammar boxes were too easy, but I guessed they would
provide exciting work for the younger ones. I added some
decorations to the interpretive-reading box, which was full
of cards describing short scenes to dramatize. Alongside it
I displayed a handmade book called "The Shape of Poetry,"
an illustrated guide to writing poems.

Science is all about exploration, so materials on several
shelves suggested many paths. On one shelf there were
rocks, books about geology, and magnifying glasses. On
another were star charts, galaxy photos, and books about
the planets. There was also lab equipment—flasks, beakers,
graduated cylinders, and test tubes—made mostly of glass.
(Montessori encourages using breakable things to help
children develop careful and purposeful handing.) And
there were the essential supplies for kitchen chemistry—
salt ($NaCl$), vinegar (CH_3COOH), oil ($C_{18}H_{34}O_2$), baking
soda ($NaHCO_3$), sugar ($C_{12}H_{22}O_{11}$), and others, all appropri-
ately labeled. I displayed a few cards with simple instructions for conducting an experiment, like observing liquid
weight.

WHICH IS HEAVIER—OIL OR WATER?

PREDICT which one is heavier.

COLLECT: tall cylinder, rubber stopper, 2 small
beakers, oil, water

DIRECTIONS:

1. Pour water into a beaker up to the first line from the bottom.
2. Fill the other one in the same way with oil.
3. Pour both liquids into the cylinder, one at a time.
4. Cap the cylinder with the stopper. Shake it.
5. Wait and watch what happens.

WRITE what you observed in your journal

Adjacent to the science shelves was a small kitchen with a large multipurpose table where experiments could be conducted, microscopes set up, plants potted. Sometimes the kitchen area would also serve as an art center, with supplies for painting and drawing and sculpting stored in the surrounding cabinets. On the kitchen walls were prints of O'Keefe's *Red Poppies*, Picasso's *Girl before a Mirror*, and Renoir's *Dance at Bougival*, reminders of art exhibits we could visit at local museums.

History shelves had a few real fossils, traceable dinosaur skeletons, and colorful folders about ancient civilizations. Geography featured landscape photography, an unusual puzzle of the world, and topography models. On the counter above these shelves was a long display unit where I posted several maps—the world, Latin America, and Japan, where I had spent two years studying Japanese education. In front of the maps I displayed some Japanese children's games, hats from Uzbekistan, a folktale from New Zealand, and a UNICEF book called *Children Just Like Me*.

What would engage my new students? I knew they would come to school eagerly, bored with summer's extravagance of free time and ready for new challenges. What kind of daily writing would be meaningful to them? What stories would stoke their imaginations? Would they be interested in hieroglyphics, the story of the United Nations, the history of zero?

The breadth of the integrated curriculum for any mixed-age class is daunting. Elementary teachers are generalists rather than specialists. Daily we field questions about a wide range of topics we know little about: How fast can a jet travel? How could I find out about my dog's breed (he's mixed)? What are some girls' names in Australia? Where is Trinidad?

In the early weeks, I often prepared a simple survey to help students get acquainted. They answered questions about the number of siblings and pets in their household, their favorite sports and hobbies, where their grandparents lived, places they had visited over the summer. By cutting up the answer sheets, I could bundle the answers to each question and ask small groups to tally the responses. Then I suggested ways to display the results—a bar graph to show numbers of siblings, a pie chart of favorite holidays, or a map showing where grandparents lived. Once, as I helped a group map grandparents' locations, I noticed someone's grandparents lived in Trinidad. I pointed out the island on our world map and recommended the group find out whose grandparents lived there. The student they identified went home with a bank of questions about Trinidad while I imagined a study of island nations. A few days later the student returned to report that her grandparents did indeed live in Trinidad—Trinidad, Colorado, that is, just an hour south of Denver.

I excused my ignorance by explaining that I was a newcomer to the state, but the incident reminded me that elementary teachers are continually humbled by what we don't know. There is no mastering the curriculum. We are always learning content on the job, taking many short trips, finding more questions than answers, and sending our student explorers on up ahead to find out more.

Like classrooms in many public schools, mine was a curious combination of old and new. On both ends were green chalkboards you could write on best with old-fashioned thick chalk, which wasn't in the school supply catalogue any longer. On a small corner table sat an old desk phone, the type with punch buttons for different lines. One triggered a school-wide alarm, easily pressed by mistake and not an uncommon event. Beside the phone was a vintage boom box that played both CDs and audiotapes. Two computers updated the picture, one set up for student use. Some children used the computer's search functions, but most preferred books. Several older students had taken keyboarding lessons with the librarian and practiced by typing final drafts of their projects or an occasional newsletter. The second computer was designated for record-keeping and sending data to the district. Whenever possible, I happily passed those jobs on to my assistant.

Tables throughout the classroom provided intersections where students could work together. I asked the custodian to lower half of them to accommodate the shorter legs of students I was expecting. Most of the tables were trapezoid-shaped, and two of them combined easily to form a hexagonal unit that seated four to six. By shifting just a few tables, we could create a central space large enough to accommodate everyone sitting on the floor in a circle. A comfortable place to gather would be essential for community meetings.

In one corner of the classroom was a small library. Bookshelves on three sides were set wide enough apart to create small sitting places in between, and a Persian rug of soft, rosy hues carpeted the middle. The famous NASA image of the cloud-bedecked earth graced the large bulletin board above the shelves. This was a place to browse, to think, sometimes simply a place to rest. It was almost always a quiet place. Reference books occupied one shelf, poetry another, but our prized collection was fiction, which had been chosen by my students one year when the district had granted every teacher $1,000 for books.

I remember clearly the morning I asked the children what we needed in our library. Hands shot up with many requests: "The complete series, please, of Lemony Snicket, the *American Girl* books, *Magic Tree House*, all of *Harry Potter*, *Warrior Cats*, the *Narnia* stories."

On a November Saturday I had gone to the bookstore and spent all the money in half an hour. And then I watched the children read. They read during silent reading, they read during noisy work periods. They constantly discussed books with one another, even starting a card file of favorite books and who would enjoy them. I should have paid better attention to their year-end reading scores to quantify the outcomes of reading immersion. What I knew for sure was that those thirty children would be readers for life.

Going out to the local library was not an option for

the classes in our school. We were located in an inner-city neighborhood with the nearest library several miles away, not safe enough or close enough for a walk. Restrictions on parents driving students anywhere were prohibitive. Fortunately, a new library wing had recently been added to our school, complete with a bank of updated computers and new books. Unfortunately, all the classes in the building used the library, some at specific times, and the librarian was part-time, so access was limited. My favorite resource in the school library was the collection of children's books in sets—five to ten copies of the same carefully chosen book. I often checked out a set for literature study with a small group.

In our classroom library I posted a map showing the locations of local libraries and shared it with parents at our first meeting, encouraging them to take their children to the library as often as possible. Some followed up on my suggestion. It seems important to remember how many children don't have access to books at home or anyone to take them to the library. Reading books online is increasingly common, but I am convinced young people need books in their hands. Browsing books, sharing them with friends, or discovering an exciting new series are childhood treasures. The school can be instrumental in assuring those experiences for every child.

On top of one shelf in our classroom library I displayed several *Magic Tree House* books and a few others with modest reading demands. I also posted one of my favorite poems on the Poetry Post, where students would be invited to display their own poems.

The adjustments I made in the room were small, each

aimed at engaging younger students. Over the next nine months I would add a few things or change a display, but most of the books and materials on the shelves would be found where they were now.

To some, such a highly organized environment seems narrow and restrictive. In fact, its comprehensiveness and predictability enhance freedom for the students. When the assistant superintendent of instruction spent an hour in our class one day, he commented on the visual clarity of the environment, remarking as he left, "I think I could learn in here."

A former student who had gone on to high school also paid us a visit and stayed to browse all morning. Then she sat down beside me and declared, "This is the most amazing place!"

I hoped my new students would eventually feel the same way.

On the first morning, they began arriving early. Several wore classic "first day of school" clothes I didn't expect to see again, and a few, like Ronnie, appeared to be in sleep clothes, hair unattended. I greeted everyone at the door as they arrived, shaking hands, introducing myself and my assistant, Kathryn.

Carl, a short second grader whose family I knew, almost dashed past me but remembered at the last minute to shake hands before proceeding expectantly into the classroom. Later I glimpsed him trying on one of the Uzbek hats. Maya was preadolescent, tall enough to look me in the eye but didn't. She mumbled her name and disappeared quickly into a gathering of girls near the table where new journals were stacked. Liam was shorter than Maya but clearly an older boy who returned my steady gaze and went directly to the library. Lydia was another tall fourth grader who introduced herself by telling me she loved math. Bella, a small girl with a bright smile, gave me a spontaneous hug before dancing into the room.

Several parents arrived with their children. Hayden's mother preceded him through the door, encouraging him to shake my hand, which he did reluctantly, head lowered. I had met them both at the back-to-school picnic and also looked at his file—divorced parents, conflicts with peers, not learning to read. He and his mother circled the room together, she in the lead. Javier's father shook my hand warmly and hugged his son before he left. Another mom shyly introduced herself and her fourth-grade daughter, telling me how much she'd heard about our school and how much Evelyn needed a new start. Then Piper arrived with her mother, who immediately spotted Hayden in the room and exploded. He had attacked her daughter in a previous class, she said loudly enough for everyone to hear, and they simply could not be in the same room again. By this time many children appeared to need some help, so I suggested she go directly to the office to make her case with the principal.

Joining the group gathered at the school supply table, I began to distribute journals, taking time to write each name in my best cursive on the covers. Bella slipped in beside me, watched me write her name, and then sat nearby practicing it repeatedly on the first page. Several older girls seemed eager to begin writing in their journals too.

I suggested they copy the date and the quote I had written on the chalkboard: "How wonderful it is that nobody need wait a single moment before starting to improve the world [Anne Frank, 1929–1945]."

Eventually boys drifted over to pick up journals, and most everyone began finding a place to settle. Suddenly a woman marched through the doorway and came directly toward me with two toddlers trailing and a young girl at her side. Her voice commanded our attention. They were new to the school, she announced. Her younger son was enrolled in a class downstairs, and Destiny, her only daughter, a fourth grader, would be joining this class. Then she left as abruptly as she had come. But Destiny continued, explaining that her whole name was Destiny Hope, that she preferred answering to her whole name, but Destiny or even just Hope would be okay. Her gaze surveyed the group, but most had lost interest and resumed their prior activities. I wrote her whole name on the cover of a journal and introduced her to Evelyn, who was sitting at a table alone. As newcomers to Montessori, they would both need lots of help getting started, and working together would make it easier. I asked Alyssa to show them around.

Alyssa was the only returning student in the group. She was a small fifth grader who had been designated as a special-needs child with learning disabilities. The principal had agreed to reassign her to my class because she had made such good progress the previous year. Alyssa's mother had been in jail for several years, and her father worked long hours. I had developed a warm relationship with her and believed we could all benefit if she became a leader in the class. Alyssa responded warmly when I asked her to help the newcomers. She steered them toward a table where they could sit together, helped them start their journals, and then conducted a brief tour of the classroom. I could see she was helping others along the way.

Piper's mother returned and said she had agreed to temporarily place her daughter in the class, but only if I promised she would be seated far away from Hayden. I gave her my word.

We gathered in a circle to play name games and talk about respect—for ourselves, each other, and the environment. I encouraged everyone to explore the classroom and work with materials they recognized. Briefly we discussed keeping track of work choices in journals, a habit most seemed to remember. As they left the gathering, I asked each student what they planned to do and made suggestions if they had no idea. Alyssa said she was going to count the big bead frame. She spent the rest of the morning off by herself, carefully completing each step in a long work she remembered perfectly.

Because it was my birthday, I had planned cupcake-decorating for the afternoon, an activity that proved to be a great social success. Everyone chose a combination of frostings and decorations from the array I laid out and began creating individual cakes. The project stretched out much longer than expected. Someone named their cupcake, and then everyone did—Fairy Garden, Rock Star, Peppermint Tent. When I suggested we gather to eat them, the children were alarmed. No one wanted to eat their cupcake! Instead, they took turns circulating through the room to admire one another's creations. I heard many compliments and friendly exchanges. As the afternoon came to an end, we gathered in a circle, and Alyssa taught everyone "You Can't Ride in My Little Red Wagon," a song she said was her favorite. She was on her way to becoming our leader.

Reflecting on the first day, I thought of Montessori's description of the developing social personality during the elementary years. Clearly friendship came first on everyone's agenda. I had seen powerful proof of this when I observed an "open" fourth-grade class in a public school for several months as a graduate student. Each day the class began with about twenty minutes of socializing—noisy greetings, lots of movement throughout the room. Gradually students chose activities from one of the learning centers and began to work in groups of two or three. When a child missed that initial social time, however, the result was often social isolation and an inability to engage in work. My observation notes from one morning describe the problem:

> Harold is arriving about fifteen minutes late—after most have settled into work. He is glancing around the classroom, trying to make eye contact with someone. Now he is circulating with a notebook in hand, looking for a group to join, but doesn't get an invitation. He chooses a book from the science center and goes off to an individual desk.
>
> Fifteen minutes have passed. Harold is up again, wandering, puts the book back, scans the room, goes to the math center close to where three other boys are working on multiplication tables. No one looks

up, and he takes his work to a table nearby. It looks like he may waste the whole morning trying to make contact.

In my new class, I would have to nurture social relationships if I expected great work. Over the next few days, I gave many small group lessons, assembling different combinations of individuals and encouraging them to do follow-up work together.

The younger students found meaningful work more easily, some working independently or connecting with a partner. Bella was delighted to remember how to multiply with the checkerboard. Piper discovered the Poetry Binder and shared it with Javier. Hayden counted several bead chains. A summary of the first week written by Carl, however, suggests that making friends was still the main thing:

Dr. Angell is my teacher.
   Today I started a story called Wicked.
   I did subtraction perfectly.
   Also I made a book mark.

My favorite things this week
   1. Making cupcakes
   2. Liam
   3. Math facts
   4. Liam
   5. Geometry

As the second week began, a low hum suggested social connections being formed. Destiny and Evelyn were now fast friends but clearly baffled by the activity around them. Exploring a classroom was outside their experience, and working without assignments made no sense at all. Alyssa continued to help. I made a list of activities I thought the three could do together, and she began several mornings demonstrating materials for the girls, but they seldom continued on their own.

Often the two newcomers drifted off to a corner, keeping their distance from the table where I gathered students for lessons. First thing one morning I insisted they come to a lesson about animals. (All kids love animals, right?) Scattering out pictures we would use later to study classification, I invited everyone to choose an animal they recognized and tell something about it. They responded with facts and stories—a big black bear encountered on a family trip to Yellowstone, caiman crocodiles living in a moat at a downtown restaurant, amazing pet tricks seen on YouTube. After several turns around the table, I solicited suggestions about how to learn more about animals. The two youngest in the group quickly announced they were going to do research on an animal no one had identified. They each chose a picture and left to get started. Others moved the remaining pictures to a mat on the floor and continued telling stories. They invited Destiny and Evelyn to join them, but the girls didn't stay with the group for long.

I had another idea. Perhaps writing letters would promote new friendships and also encourage the girls to write. (Who hasn't passed a note to a friend?) Indeed, I thought everyone would benefit from an activity that invited self-expression. So I gathered the group for letter-writing, passing out special paper and suggesting each person write to someone in the class they would like to know better. I had posted a list of their names.

Everyone followed along as I explained the form and composed my own letter at the easel—date and salutation (with a comma), a paragraph about themselves, and a second one with questions for the recipient. Evelyn and Destiny were both writing. When we had added a closing and most were finished, I demonstrated how to fold the paper in thirds, seal it with a colored circle sticker, and add the addressee's name on the front. Then I pointed out a landmark—a mailbox installed on the end of a tall shelf where their letters should be deposited. Alyssa distributed the mail at the end of the day.

First thing next morning Destiny and Evelyn were at my table asking if they could write more letters. Of course I said yes, and they were off, taking several sheets of letter-writing paper and a page of stickers with them. A number of girls and a few boys followed suit, and by late afternoon the mailbox was stuffed. Mail distribution at the end of the day was a big event, and receiving a letter invited a response. The newcomers had found a reason to work.

Writing letters continued to be a popular activity throughout the year. Several times the students voted to shut down the mailbox temporarily because of disrespectful content or the absence of proper form, which was poorly regarded. However, letters often helped resolve conflict. A good letter of apology was usually accepted.

After the first two weeks, children were greeting

each other warmly in the morning. The hum in the room increased in volume sprinkled with occasional laughter. One afternoon I invited everyone to complete the Get-Acquainted Survey so that we could learn about each other's siblings and pets and favorite holidays and sports and hobbies. Small groups worked together to count the responses, made graphs or charts to show the results, and shared their findings. One group volunteered to combine all the displays on a big poster, which they entitled Who We Are.

2 September
The Storyteller

The secret of good teaching is to regard the child's intelligence as a fertile field in which seeds may be sown, to grow under the heat of flaming imagination.

—Maria Montessori[1]

Storytelling launches the elementary curriculum, which Dr. Montessori called cosmic education. It is framed by five stories told to strike the imagination: the origin of the universe, the evolution of plants and animals on earth, the coming of humans, the invention of the alphabet, and the story of mathematics. Some teachers tell all five during the first week of school, but spreading them out always worked better for me. Because elementary children are hero-worshippers, they also love to hear stories about great and unknown people, tales weaving human endeavor and marvelous events together. We must call attention to men and women hidden from the light of fame, wrote Montessori, so that children will develop a love for humanity.[2]

A few days before I told the first story of the big bang, I invited the children to spend a morning doing simple experiments. Liam and Carl had visited the science shelves, but most avoided the area. Briefly I explained how to conduct the experiments set up around the room—making mixtures, watching the attraction of torn paper bits on the surface of water, discovering gravity in a sand-filled dishpan with Ping-Pong balls and a few steel bolts. Each experiment introduced a concept they would hear more about in the story. I suggested no more than three students work together at a station. Each was furnished with the necessary equipment and instructions ending with "Reset for the next person." There was a buzz of activity all morning.

During lunchtime, I returned all the equipment to their proper places on the science shelves. When the afternoon work period began, however, several children located and reassembled the equipment needed to repeat an experiment. Among them were Destiny and Evelyn, who chose mixtures.

For the next several days, they made mixtures almost nonstop. At first they followed the original experiment instructions, filling identical tumblers with equal amounts of water, adding sugar to one and cornstarch to the other, stirring, watching the sugar water become clear and the other stay cloudy, waiting three minutes, and then tasting both liquids. The second day they proposed new ingredients for the mixtures such as soap powder, baking soda, baby powder, salt. They seemed to especially like cleaning up after each experiment, washing the tumblers and carefully returning the ingredients and equipment to their proper places. On several occasions they put everything back and then got it all out to try the experiment again.

Destiny and Evelyn were behaving like preschoolers

Montessori had often described—persisting, repeating, and housekeeping—totally unaware of what went on around them. A small group began sculpting a clay volcano at the same table where the girls were working, but the two continued making mixtures.

When the volcano was completed and mostly dried out, it was time to tell the story.

We gathered on the floor around a big tarp, the volcano in the center. With my most dramatic voice, I began describing the vastness of cold space where infinite zero energy bubbled just enough to make a seed, a tiny bit of radiation that exploded and expanded so fast there was no way for it to get back together again. Faster than the speed of light, the universe expanded to one hundred trillion times its original size. Billions of galaxies went spinning out into space in such a way that they would never collide, our Milky Way just one of them. I told about Galileo and the first telescope, the red shift, the gravitational fields that pulled planets to stars like our sun, the amazing dance of elements transforming earth from a blazing star to a planet, and the era of volcanoes (here the model exploded on cue.)

And then my favorite line, "The smoke from the volcanoes encircled the earth, hiding it from the sun, and after millions and millions of years, it began to rain."

Montessori's impressionistic charts help dramatize the story, the final one a simple picture of Earth as a half-sphere with land and water and air and sun, ready for life. My concluding remarks swept across the first mixtures, proteins, cells, animals, plants, and humans. I think I told the story under thirty minutes. Everyone gasped and giggled when the volcano exploded, and a few children nodded knowingly when I alluded to gravity or mixtures. But when I finished, there was a hush.

I left them sitting together for a moment, long enough to punch Play on the boom box cued up for Jim Post's song "The Galaxy / Lighten Up." They listened closely the first time through, and then I handed out song sheets so we could join in the chorus together:

> Just remember that you're standing on a planet
> that's evolving
> And revolving at 900 miles an hour
> It's orbiting at 90 miles a second, so it's reckoned
> Round the sun that is the source for all our pow'r
> The sun and you and me and all the stars that we
> can see
> Are moving at a million miles a day
> In an outer spiral arm at 40,000 miles an hour
> In a galaxy we call the Milky Way[3]

As the song played on, I sent everyone off to create collages with torn construction paper scraps I had placed on each table. I suggested illustrating the part of the story they liked best and then writing a sentence somewhere on the picture to describe it. As each child finished, I asked permission to display their collage on the wall. Soon most were milling around, looking closely at others' images.

Destiny and Evelyn were stalled. They sat at a table watching others tearing and pasting, unable to get started.

As the afternoon wound down, I did notice them browsing among the artistic renderings with the others.

Next morning the two girls were in the kitchen first thing again, but instead of making mixtures, they were making collages. They worked side by side nearly all morning, tearing up colored paper and pasting pieces together.

In another part of the classroom, Carl was busy making a book of planets. He began with a drawing of Mars, adding a few facts at the bottom of the page. By the time he had gone on to Jupiter, Liam and two others had joined the project, each working on a planet Carl assigned. They continued for several days with a gathering of many books, a flurry of drawings, and animated discussions about sizes and distances and surface temperatures. In the end, some parts couldn't be located, but the book had a page for every planet and several more. It landed on the science shelf for all to enjoy.

I always hope there will be one or two, maybe even several, students whose imagination catches fire quickly and burns so brightly that their enthusiasm spreads. I think of these children as sparks, and Carl clearly was one.

While the planet project was underway, Liam began reading a book about Galileo. Hayden was making telescopes. Most of the others, however, returned to their previous endeavors. Two younger girls were intent on studying King Tut (the exhibit was in town), Piper was writing a report about George Washington, and Martin was gathering facts about Jackie Robinson. It seems they had moved on to hero-worshipping.

I decided to postpone the evolution stories and provide instead an overview of recorded history. Gathering everyone together, I introduced the Clock of Eras, a chart representing the 4.5 billion years since the big bang on a twelve-hour clock. Each hour represents about four hundred million years. The first four hours are black to suggest the period of earth's formation, and then comes a long six-hour period when life began with proteins and the first simple cells. The story of evolution gets exciting during the Paleozoic hour and a half when there was an explosion of life in the seas. Subsequent periods get increasingly shorter—the Mesozoic era of dinosaurs, the Cenozoic era of mammals, and, finally, the Neozoic era, when humans appeared. The stories of recorded history I was about to tell occurred during the last half-minute on the Clock of Eras. That always makes a big impression.

We imagined stretching those last thirty seconds out on a line as I rolled out the Timeline of Centuries. It is a long strip marked off in inches labeled with numbers for the centuries from 10,000 BCE to the present. The first long section representing the centuries before zero is green, and the latter part is red. I told a story about Julius Caesar's frustrations with a calendar that failed to predict the seasons accurately, resulting in defeats to his armies. Subsequent consultations with his astronomer gave us the 365-day year and leap years. I described the Christian monks who established the birth of Jesus as the year zero, defining the periods BC (Before Christ) and AD (Anno Domini) that were later renamed BCE (Before the Common Era), and CE. Together we named the centuries forward and backward from zero, planting little tickets on each one as we counted them.

When we gathered around the Timeline of Centuries again, I told stories about great milestones of civilization, placing simple drawings on the timeline to indicate when each occurred. There were the handprints on the walls of the Lascaux cave, the Sumerian ziggurat, Egyptian hieroglyphs, the Phoenician alphabet, a Greek temple, illumination on a medieval manuscript, Michelangelo's sketch of a flying machine, George Washington, the Apollo II landing on the moon, and, finally, our class.

The Timeline of Centuries remained on display for several weeks. It was one of the permanent installations in the elementary class I had observed in Bergamo, where it extended the length of the classroom on a low table along one wall. That timeline had similar illustrations spaced farther apart because of its length, which further dramatized the slow progression of civilization until recent times. Often I observed children walking slowly all along it. In our classroom I had drawn the icons on separate cards with dates on the back so that students could practice locating them on the timeline. Within the week, several students added their own illustrated cards to the collection. Jackie Robinson's first game as a Brooklyn Dodger in 1947 was one of them.

Soon I assembled a small group for the history of transportation by water, using a folder of pictures, labels (with dates), and short stories designed for younger students. Most read the stories easily and then worked together to locate the pictures on the timeline—the raft, the canoe, the Egyptian ship that could only sail before the wind, the ships Phoenicians built to navigate in any direction, the Roman warships, the caravel, the clipper ships, the steamboat, the aircraft carrier, the submarine.

At the end of the lesson, Javier announced that he

was going to study the history of airplanes. He enlisted a friend to help, and together they quickly found a book about the Wright brothers and a long encyclopedia article about aircraft. Javier began detailed drawings of planes, each labeled with a name and date and a few key facts. His companion retired from the project at the end of a week, but Javier stayed with the theme all year long. He drew blimps and jets and spacecraft. He read fiction and nonfiction about airplanes and famous flyers. When his parents announced they were flying the family to Puerto Rico over the holiday break, he was "over the moon."

I assembled several girls to talk about the history of clothing. Destiny and Evelyn were in the group. So was Lydia, the most admired fourth-grade girl in the class who seemed surprised by her peers' esteem but eager to live up to their expectations. I had noticed fashion drawings in her journal. Together we examined a similar set of picture-story cards—Egyptians with pleated skirts, Phoenicians in purple, Greek drapes, Renaissance finery, and modern fashion.

When the discussion concluded, Lydia left for the main library to find out more about the history of fashion. She returned with a book about Egypt and started drawing. Soon, however, other interests eclipsed her project. She was excited about long division and loved doing animal reports with friends. Nevertheless, without any prompting, Lydia tackled a new era about once a month. During the very last week of school, she presented her report with a long timeline of changing fashions through history. Although her engagement lacked Javier's passion, that thread of research seemed to give Lydia's journey focus.

On Wednesday mornings I became an official observer for thirty minutes. Perched on the special visitor's chair with clipboard in hand, I watched the class intently and took notes. Usually I was impressed by the diversity of work going on. A few students still flitted from one activity to the next. Observing often improved everyone's work ethic, a subtle shift I also noticed when walking around the room with a camera.

I reserved Thursday afternoons for individual conferences, a time to review students' work, make suggestions, and plan lessons together. Some students needed a conference every week, others only occasionally.

I met individually with Destiny and Evelyn every week, listening for sparks of interest and trying to fan those flames. When it became clear neither would take a chance with the hands-on math materials, I pointed out the fourth-grade math textbook on the shelf and found content within each girl's reach. I introduced Evelyn to the grammar boxes with some success, and she shared them with Destiny. They continued to stick together.

I told stories at every opportunity. With small groups of younger students, I introduced the geography charts that continue the story of earth's formation. When the autumnal equinox arrived, I gathered the whole class to explain the changing seasons. With the sun chart in the middle, I walked around with the globe to dramatize earth's revolution, using clock time to describe the points at which each new season begins. In the discussion that followed, it became clear that many didn't understand how to tell time from the analog clock on the wall. When I asked about the timekeeping they were doing in their journals, several reported they asked friends what time it was or just guessed.

Yes, I was chagrined. I had used the clock to explain earth's history and introduced the concept of centuries, but many didn't know how to tell time.

I quickly located some clock stamps and showed several students how to make a timeline of their day with multiple stamps on a long strip. I began drawing clocks on the chalkboard to show times for special events and bought a telling-time bingo game to play on Friday afternoons. I also suggested stamping clocks in journals to keep an accurate record of work.

Carl began stamping in his journal regularly, tracking every activity by the minute. I counted eighteen clock stamps for one day in November. Once again, his enthusiasm inspired others, including Evelyn and Destiny. Keeping track of time with clock stamps seemed to help the girls stay at work.

It was time to start reading stories together.

In mid-September I organized literature study groups, inviting several students to read the same book and come together to discuss it. The composition of the groups was based partly on reading ability but also shared interests and social compatibility.

One group was a mix of boys and girls including Piper, who had suggested reading *Because of Winn-Dixie* by Kate DiCamillo. At our first meeting I learned that most of them had either heard the book read aloud or had seen the movie, but all seemed eager to read the story again. Because they already understood the plot, they appreciated other aspects of the story. Most wrote good questions for our discussions and often made insightful comments about the characters.

I invited Alyssa, Maya, Lydia, Destiny, and Evelyn—each girl somewhat unsure of her reading ability—to tackle *The Music of Dolphins* together. It is the story of a twelve-year-old girl rescued from a life spent living with dolphins and the professionals who try to civilize her and teach her to speak. They name her Mila. To illustrate the painfully slow process of acquiring language, the early pages of the book have only a few words and repetitive phrases. Subsequent short chapters expand gradually to include more vocabulary and complex constructions until the middle chapters tell the story at a third- or fourth-grade reading level.

I asked the girls to read a few chapters before each meeting, but we often read them aloud when we met. We moved slowly, dissecting the meanings of each sentence and new words in Mila's vocabulary. The girls became more confident and begged to read farther ahead. Destiny and Evelyn began to read previous chapters aloud to each other.

Halfway through the book, a sympathetic character introduces Mila to Paul Winter's "Music of the Dolphins," which includes the recorded cries and songs of dolphins. When I played some of this music for the group, the whole class stopped to listen. Afterward others asked to hear about the story and more of the music.

At a class meeting, someone suggested we play Winter's music regularly during lunch cleanup, and all agreed. Listening to the dolphin music transformed a typically noisy time of day into an orderly set of routine tasks undertaken in slow motion, imitating the grace and quiet of the great animals. The restrained cleanup routine persisted through-out the school year, whenever the music was played.

I organized another group of boys whose reading skills were mixed—Carl, Javier, and Ronnie among them. The book *Year of the Panda* tells the story of a boy in China rescuing and temporarily adopting a baby panda. The text demands are modest, but the story's theme of endangered species prompted good conversations.

Three book groups were meeting regularly, but I had not included everyone. Liam and a few others were constantly engrossed in reading good books. Several younger girls were so busy with other pursuits that it seemed wrong to add a book study to their agendas. Then, late in the month, we had our first class visit to the school library. Halfway through the hour, the girls came to me with identical books in hand. Bella, the youngest of the group, did the talking, explaining that she had found enough copies of a book called *The Secret School* for all the girls who weren't in a literature study group yet. She had gathered them together, and they had agreed to form their own group. Would I like to join?

Bella was another spark.

3 October
The Companion

Let us wait, and be always ready to share in both the joys and the difficulties which the children experience…to treat them as we should like to be treated ourselves—not to be disturbed in our work, not to find hindrances to our efforts, to have good friends ready to help us in times of need, to see them rejoice with us, to be on terms of equality with them, to be able to confide and trust in them—this is what we need for happy companionship.

—Maria Montessori[1]

Of course, I was delighted to accept Bella's invitation to join the club. She decided how far we should read ahead in *The Secret School,* posting the page number and next meeting time on the board right under my listings for other book groups. The spontaneous formation of the new book club was evidence of self-directed learning. In fact, many children were exploring, moving forward on unique journeys. They would only need me as an occasional companion.

With others still finding their way, I worked on building

relationships. Maya often refused invitations to lessons, sticking doggedly to multiplication tables at a single remote desk. How could I penetrate that defensiveness and get her to trust my good intentions? How could I connect with Ellie who spent half her time in the special education room and had trouble engaging when she returned to our classroom? How could I help Blake get interested in something besides reading—and should I? How could I persuade Laura, a second-language learner, to slow down when she told me her stories and let me help her learn to write using the conventions of the English language? How could I get Ronnie to care about something he had not seen in a video game? He was starting to look like a drop-out waiting to happen. How do you follow a child—or go along—when they appear to be going nowhere?

Helping children like Maya and Ronnie sent me searching for more information about their home life and prior experience. Dr. Montessori asserted that each individual's intelligence, which she called the psyche (P), is an interaction between internal experience (I) and environmental stimuli (E), or $P = I \times E$. It is now widely understood that early experience figures heavily in a child's school success, but comparisons of student achievement seldom take that factor into account. With regard to testing, Dr. Montessori recommended that it would be better to measure the methods used to educate rather than presuming to measure the unknown.[2]

I learned more about Ronnie's prior experience when I met with his grandfather. Ronnie's mother lived in a nearby town but had turned him over to her parents when he was about one. She hadn't seen him much since then. Ronnie still lived with his grandmother, an artist presently recovering from brain surgery, and this young grandfather, who seemed baffled by his role as primary caregiver for his grown daughter's eight-year-old son. He had recently lost his job staying home too often to take care of the grandmother, and their financial situation was perilous. One Friday afternoon, Ronnie's mother showed up unexpectedly to take him home with her for the weekend. It was no surprise that the following Monday he was totally disconnected. Ronnie needed my companionship full time. We began to meet every day first thing to plan his day, and he often stayed by my side to work.

A few of the students' folders passed on to me from previous teachers proved helpful, but individual conferences gave me more insight into that unknown factor, the internal landscape of previous experience. Maya told me her father had been insisting she memorize the multiplication tables since she began grade school. He quizzed her every day, but she never could remember them fast enough. We agreed that learning to multiply with double-digit multipliers might help, and she allowed me to introduce her to the checkerboard.

Ellie had been working on addition in her special education class, but she said she wanted to learn long division with the test tubes. There were a dozen lessons on my list for her before long division, but we sat together for several days until she could manipulate all the parts and arrive at a quotient. She worked at it for the rest of the year until she had mastered the most advanced applications.

When I had a long talk with Blake, he confessed he had once spent lots of time learning about geometry but had forgotten everything he knew. Together we made a plan to review the geometry nomenclature.

Laura slowed down and let me know she wanted to learn how to make a pie graph like the one she saw in her book about Honduras, where her father had spent most of his lifetime.

When students began to accept me as a companion, they often shared their parents' expectations. Unlike Maya's father, who worried about his daughter falling behind in math, Martin's parents saw him as a math whiz. He responded by devoting himself to proving them right. He was the only student I've ever known who repeated, at least three times during the year, all of the steps for transposing the bead bar display of the multiplication tables into the tower of cubes—an exercise we called the bead decanomial. During one open house, he tried to squeeze in a demonstration of the whole thing for his parents in sixty minutes.

Isabella's parents feared she would never be good at math, so new math work for her was always accompanied with a kind of personal panic, no matter how much assurance or support I provided. Isabella was a second-language learner who often hovered on the periphery of small group work. When I was able to coax her into working more independently, she was often amazed by what she was able to do on her own. Private lessons worked best for Isabella; she needed a very personal kind of companionship.

Lessons with just two or three individuals sometimes helped build relationships. I assembled Liam and Blake and Camilla, all devout readers, for a geometry lesson about lines—horizontal, vertical, and oblique. At its conclusion, the two boys went off together and began an imaginative series of line drawings. They were back at my table in three days, asking for another lesson, and continued to pursue the geometry curriculum with minimal help. When we did meet, they often surprised me with their discoveries before asking, "What's next?" We became good friends.

Camilla, however, was not impressed with lines or geometry. She made a booklet about lines and then got lost in another book. Camilla read fiction, nonfiction, and biographies. With each new book, she appeared totally engaged, reading from beginning to end in every spare moment, a pattern that persisted throughout the year. Who could complain?

Piper was our resident poet with a fierce independence suggesting she didn't need a companion. She encouraged me to start a poetry club, which began meeting on Tuesday afternoons. Participants, mostly girls, read their favorite poems to each other or shared poems they had written. Piper's poems were usually personal—about her mother, her dog, or her wishes. Occasionally she composed a melody for one of her poems and invited a few girls to learn the song. They practiced in the hallway, and at the end of an afternoon there would be a performance of Piper's latest. Bella, who had already announced her plans to be a diva, was an enthusiastic participant. Evelyn and Destiny were usually happy to be backup singers. I was always pleased to see them interacting with others.

One day they showed up at my table with a set of small boxes they had found on the math shelf. Each was filled with some kind of trinket—multicolored paper clips, beads of different shapes, river stones. When counted and sorted, these objects provided data for bar graphs. We started with the box of paper clips, sorting them into color piles. I showed the girls how to construct the x and y axis on graph paper and how to draw colored bars representing the number of clips in each pile.

One brief lesson was all they needed. They went immediately to work making more bar graphs and soon shared the activity with Maya and Piper, who were also intrigued. For a week the four worked with the contents of the boxes, going back several times to sort the paper clips. It was the first time I had seen Maya truly engaged.

Then the girls began to collect their own data by interviewing peers about favorite sports and foods and TV shows. One morning I managed to gather them up to introduce the idea of central tendency. In subsequent class presentations, they sometimes reported the mode or median of their data collection, suggesting they understood how those statistics added interest to their conclusions.

More students seemed engaged each day, but several curricular areas remained unexplored. Companionship was developing between me and almost all the students. Perhaps they would trust me now to widen their interests.

On Thursday mornings the day began with an awkward forty-minute period between arrival and a gym class, just enough time to get started and then interrupted, or a reason not to get started at all. It was frustrating for everyone, so I began assembling the whole group during that time for animal classification. Usually I taught this sequence of lessons to fourth graders, many of whom had worked previously with the animal-classification charts in lower elementary classes. Few in this group had seen the charts, so the lessons engaged everyone's attention.

Understanding a classification system is a basic skill, and familiarity with the animal kingdom helps prepare students for the story of evolution on the Timeline of Life. I began with invertebrates and vertebrates because classifying animals based on the absence or presence of backbones is an easy distinction for younger students. The more scientific divisions of non-chordates and chordates can be introduced with the more advanced lessons on the vital functions.

In each subsequent lesson I introduced a phylum of invertebrates, writing the name and definition on the easel for the students to copy. On a central table I displayed every picture I could find of representative animals so that students could choose a picture they liked and add a drawing to their page. Drawing from a reference rather than relying on memory or imagination was an important part of the work, new to many. After each lesson the students stored the new page they had created in a red folder that kept their animal-classification work together.

Everyone enjoyed the work, even Hayden who had been reluctant to participate in any group activity. Now on Thursday mornings he appeared eager to begin. The lessons were mostly about drawing, and Hayden was, in my private catalogue of classroom characters, our artist-in-residence. Former teachers and our team of special educators saw him differently. He had been labeled a high-risk child who was "behind."

I tried to remember my promise to separate Hayden

from Piper, whose mother had not complained again, even when I had to evacuate the room because Hayden started throwing chairs. That day I had asked my assistant, Kathryn, to lead all the other children out of the classroom and down to the library before calling the principal for help. Neither of us could calm him down, so she called Hayden's mother, who couldn't get him to leave the classroom with her. Finally we called the district's security guard. When he arrived, Hayden complied with his uniformed directives and left with his mother, but the next day he was back in his seat, cheerfully drawing.

Early in the year, when I called Hayden over for a reading assessment, he had looked at me as though shocked by my obvious mistake and exclaimed, "Oh, I can't read!" As I watched him use reference books and other materials to support his drawings, however, I noticed that he was often gathering facts from text.

Animal-classification lessons gave Hayden a chance to shine. His drawings were accurate and much admired by his peers. At my insistence, which included a threat of missing gym, Hayden also did the writing for each page. It was difficult to think of myself as Hayden's companion. He seemed to need distance from any and all adults.

Alyssa was eager to repeat the work of animal classification. To my dismay, however, the special education staff decided that she would fall behind if she were the only fifth grader in the class and insisted she be transferred. Alyssa continued to visit us every Friday at lunchtime. It was hard for me to believe that her academic progress would have been stunted by remaining at the top of a class for a year.

When a new third grader, an African American boy

transferring from another school, joined the class, animal classification was his answer to belonging. By the second week he had begun making a book about how animals defend themselves. Each page had a drawing of an animal with a word or two below describing their means of defense: *fangs, camouflage, sharp claws.* Soon Carl was designing pages for the book, and a new friendship began.

Animal-classification lessons engaged everyone. When the schedule of special classes changed in the second semester, assigning us art in the middle of Thursday afternoon, I rescheduled the lessons for the end of that day.

Montessori emphasized the need for uninterrupted work periods, recommending at least three continuous hours for students to become self-directed. Providing long work periods was difficult at our school because interruptions were commonplace. To meet union requirements, teacher's planning time was provided by art and music lessons, a library hour, and two 50-minute gym periods weekly. The school schedule was also littered with interruptions—assemblies for fund-raising, eye and ear screenings, official photography days, fire drills, tornado watches, and sometimes visiting performances by a traveling opera company or a string quartet—many worthy and probably necessary interruptions, but each one an intrusion on the extended work period.

One semester I studied how students spent time at school, rigorously logging the hours and minutes every day. I found the average time available for academic work, which is usually referred to as "instructional time," to be a discouraging 12.87 hours per week. That is less than three hours a day, and those hours were seldom continuous. Although I had set out to investigate the scarcity of instructional time, what I found was a scarcity of learning time. (http://time-toteach.wordpress.com/2009/02/01)

I often took small groups to the garden, where we found companionship in all the ordinary tasks of digging, weeding, and watering. Basil was our main crop, and in early October we harvested the last of it. I brought in my favorite pesto recipe, a blender, and pasta so we could prepare a communal lunch. Sometimes Kathryn went to the garden with a few children. On several days, they returned with bunches of chocolate mint leaves and made tea for everyone.

However, opportunities for garden work were on the wane. To promote continuing interest in botany, on several Friday afternoons I showed segments of the BBC series *The Private Life of Plants*. Narrated by David Attenborough and replete with awe-inspiring time-lapse photography, the videos always drew a crowd. I also brought in several plants that could be harvested for cuttings, a spider plant and several hardy succulents. Evelyn and Destiny took immediate interest in starting their own plants. Bella joined them with a few pointers on how best to proceed.

I also used a botany theme for the first homework assignment, which asked students to adopt a tree near their home. The instructions were to find a tree, draw it, and write observations. Several times during the year the homework included visiting the adopted trees to observe changes, make drawings, and collect samples.

Although homework is not often part of a Montessori

program, I came to believe it served many purposes for the students at our school. Children like Destiny and Maya spent long hours in day care after school, and homework was their best option. Activities I suggested for homework gave students something to talk about at day care, to argue about on the bus, to chat about on their telephones, to look up on home computers. Parents appreciated homework because it provided an alternative to TV or video games. It also gave them a window on their children's work at school. For example, when we began discussing the United Nations, homework included interviewing someone in the family about the biggest problems in the world. I hoped these kinds of assignments would encourage parents to begin asking their children "What are you learning?" instead of "How are you doing?"

Homework folders went off with the students on Monday afternoon. Enclosed was a guide sheet with four assignments: a spelling list and a page of math facts (both chosen by the students) and two content-related questions or small projects. The folders were due back on Friday morning.

When I explained the homework program, Destiny had raised her hand and inquired, "What are you going to do if I don't do my homework?"

"I won't give you any more," I replied.

"That's the stupidest thing I ever heard of!" she muttered loud enough for most of us to hear.

However, it was easy to stay true to my word. When a homework folder wasn't returned, there was simply nothing to fill for the next week. It took Destiny about three weeks to start returning her homework folder, incomplete at first, but then it was there in the basket almost every Friday. Doing your homework was a way of participating, being part of the group. As homework folders arrived, I often posted the variety of responses to an inquiry. Almost everyone looked forward to Friday spelling tests. Several of the youngest girls seldom did homework and didn't join in until the very end of the year. Spelling tests were a social event, and they had better things to do on Friday mornings.

Despite my display of maps and artifacts from other countries, geography was another curricular area getting little attention. In one particularly memorable lecture during my training, Camillo Grazzini presented a diagram of the elementary curriculum he had developed with Mario, Dr. Montessori's son. At its center was geography with all the other subjects arrayed around it. This was geography understood in its broadest sense—the study of places, people, and cultures and all the implied relationships.

The birthday of the United Nations on October 24 presented an opportunity to bring geography into the classroom conversation. Although many doubt the effectiveness of the UN, it is difficult to dispute the worthiness of its goals or to imagine our world without it. In Montessori's 1936 address before the European congress for peace in Brussels, she called for nations to come together as a great nation of humanity. One way for children to understand that idea is by recognizing the similarity of people's needs, a concept introduced with a chart called the Fundamental Needs of Humans. It would serve as an organizer for research about other countries.

One morning I read aloud the list of the 190 UN member nations, which set off a rash of mapmaking activities. Black-line maps of the continents were called up for action. Some students worked with the map of continents, but most focused on one continent, coloring each country and writing its name, sometimes identifying topographical features or capital cities. The maps I had displayed along the counter got more attention, and so did the artifacts gathering dust in front of them. One day Carl and Javier wore the hats from Uzbekistan all morning.

I suggested everyone choose one country to study, individually or with a partner. Most wanted their own country. Uzbekistan was chosen quickly along with Japan, Mexico, France, and China. Some students were eager to find out about a country no one had ever heard of—Nepal, Botswana, Tajikistan. Others chose a country with ties to their family history. Destiny, Evelyn, Maya, and Hayden each selected a country to represent but limited their projects to painting the country's flag. Everyone else seemed eager to write a report or do a big project.

To help students launch their projects, I introduced the chart of basic human needs, which is divided into physical and spiritual domains. Pictures on one side of the chart show how humans meet their needs for transportation, housing, clothing, food, and shelter. On the other side are pictures representing the need for language, art, culture, religion, and vanity, humans' need to decorate themselves. In a follow-up discussion of the chart, I introduced the concept of culture as the unique composite of ways people meet their needs—how they build their homes; how they cook their meals; how they educate their young; how they go places; how they represent their world in paintings, music, and body decorations; how they worship.

When we gathered to make up research questions, the students were quick to respond. I listed their suggestions on a big chart: Where is my country? What is the weather like? Their homes? Their clothing? Their schools? What is their religion? What are their favorite holidays? What are their favorite sports? (Many questions sounded like the classroom surveys.) Do they have good hospitals? What are they proud of in their history? Why would you want to visit there? The list of questions remained on the wall throughout the research and report-writing cycle. Whenever students launched subsequent research projects, I reminded them to begin by writing a list of their questions.

I encouraged finding answers in books or by talking to people who had been in the country. I pointed out the UNICEF publications and another excellent book called *Material World.*[3] In it families from countries around the world are pictured standing in front of their houses surrounded by all the possessions usually kept inside. Their things are numbered in the photos and named in the text with little additional commentary, but the photographs speak for themselves.

A file box on the shelf contained index cards cut in half. I encouraged students to use the cards when they found answers to their questions, writing only one note on each card for later sorting. There were also envelopes for keeping notes together.

I started a project of my own to stay out of their way. I began reading about the Convention on the Rights of the Child. Adopted in 1989 by the UN General Assembly, the United States has failed for more than twenty years to ratify this powerful document protecting the human rights of children worldwide. Only two other nations have refused to sign on—Somalia and South Sudan. My research questions focused on the history of US resistance to this document.

While the research projects were underway, students took turns painting large flags for their country. I taught a song called "Teaching Peace" accompanied by sign language and also a simple Japanese fan dance that mimics the activities of rice cultivation. One day I read aloud *Hiroshima No Pika*, a children's book illustrating the human tragedy that ended a war and renewed the world's commitment to peace.

Individual projects progressed steadily. When someone spilled their notes out on the table or floor, a sorting process ensued. Which ones went together? Some might describe the country's geography. Another category might be jobs people do or favorite children's activities or traditions. By creating small piles of notes that seemed to belong together, students began to see each pile as a new paragraph. Some attention was given to the logical order of the paragraphs (but not much) before the piles turned into written compositions. I asked questions about their notes, sometimes suggested more research, but more often expressed genuine interest in what they had learned. That's what companions do.

A few children asked me to read their reports to help

them find spelling errors or suggest improvements in organization. I was always happy to listen to their drafts or check their spelling, but editing and rewriting a final draft were meaningful steps for very few—mostly the older students. Liam and Blake both typed a final version of their report.

Many children found interesting ways of extending their research. Javier built a model of a Mexican adobe house. Lydia and Maya found traditional clothing to wear, and several others served ethnic food from their country when presenting reports. Almost everyone created a poster board displaying a map they had drawn along with their drawings of houses or famous monuments or symbols of the country.

Before anyone made a presentation to the class, I suggested practicing with a friend—reading the report aloud, wearing their costume, explaining the poster board, soliciting questions or comments, and finally asking a few prepared questions. Practicing improved the chances the audience would listen and learn from the presentations. Getting comments from the audience was always a favorite part for the presenter along with the final step of asking questions to find out who had been listening carefully.

The group could only sit still for one or two reports at a time. Fortunately, while many students completed the project in two weeks or less, others needed three or four weeks, and Ronnie needed two months. That spread the presentations out, and gradually the group became better at listening and learning from each other.

Quyen's project was her home country, Vietnam. She completed it in one week and then began a report about Cambodia, working methodically through the steps, taking better notes, practicing better English in her writing, and carefully completing a second display board. By the end of October she had gone on to a report about Arizona and had begun a study of pandas with a friend. Scaffolding the research process had given her everything she needed to inquire about the world.

We invited parents to join us on October 24, United Nations Day. Our program began with a parade of flags, the students processing around the room, singing many verses of "It's a Small World," followed by a roll call of nations present. We sang about peace and honored the Japanese with our dance. I read aloud a story about the founding of the United Nations while small groups portrayed the key ideas as human sculptures. We sang "Happy Birthday" to the United Nations, and then several students served snacks typical of their countries' cuisine.

In the following months, we often sang "Teaching Peace" before lunch, and the Japanese rice-planting dance became a Friday-afternoon favorite. Singing and dancing with the children were my favorite ways to enjoy their companionship.

Taken together, the group activities we shared in connection with the United Nations reminded me why I had so often built curriculum around this theme in October. It invited a conversation about people around the world and how much we have in common, especially the shared longing for world peace. It also provided a set of skills for inquiry and broadened students' interests.

4 November
The Community Organizer

A second side of education at this age concerns the children's exploration of the moral field, discrimination between good and evil...As moral activity develops, he wants to use his own judgment, which will often be quite different from that of his teachers.

—Maria Montessori[1]

I expected more peace after the United Nations activities, but there were disputes on the playground and reports of name-calling in the classroom. Destiny and Evelyn engaged sporadically in productive work but still found time to distract peers with social antics. Small groups were forming spontaneously around common interests, but others felt excluded. A few angry letters shut down the mailbox, and the usual enemies of community advanced on us—frustration, disrespect, competition, conflict.

During the first months we convened occasional meetings to discuss problems, but the group had not been very successful at resolving them. I kept an agenda sheet on the bulletin board where students could write down their concerns. The list had been blank for weeks, but now new items were being added. There was the problem of being interrupted while working. There was the problem of bad language. And, appearing more than once on the list was the problem of people getting left out. It was time for the group to confront these problems.

In early meetings I had acted as both leader and secretary, introducing some simple procedures. The group agreed on a few rules for discussions such as refraining from using people's names. They practiced making motions and several ways of voting. They discussed where to go on our two allotted field trips, agreeing on a concert in November and a trip to the Museum of Nature and Science in January.

At one meeting there had been a lively discussion of an agenda item that read "Making fun of people's work." After several bitter complaints were registered and examples given, someone suggested we needed some class rules to prevent bad behavior. Liam raised his hand and suggested our first rule: "Don't be a jerk by making fun of someone's work." The vote was unanimous in favor of the rule. Soon several other rhyming rules were adopted: "Be fair," "Use only your share," and "Be the friend you want to be; we can all be friends as you can see." Everyone was enthusiastic about the rules. Piper listed them on a wall chart, and I often heard students refer to a rule when trying to work out interpersonal conflict.

The problem of interfering with other people's work continued to be a source of frustration, one not easily solved under the existing rules. At one meeting there was general agreement that everyone should be doing serious work every day, which they defined as some math and a word study, a dictionary exercise we had practiced. They agreed you could ask someone interrupting your work if they had done both.

At another meeting the topic was cliques. There had been many suggestions about how to prevent hurt feelings and strong advocacy for inclusiveness.

Despite the occasional success in consensus-building, however, serious debate in the meetings was rare. And I had not succeeded in turning over the role of leader. Liam had tried leading one meeting, but it became unruly. No one else wanted the job. As I observed the growing social distress in November, it was clear that frequent and better class meetings were essential to the health and welfare of the community.

It was time for me to think like a community organizer. To restart our social engine, I scheduled class meetings four days a week, starting with a midmorning meeting on Monday that featured a snack. I insisted the oldest students take turns leading, calling the meeting to order, and asking for a volunteer to read the minutes, which were much shorter because meetings only lasted about fifteen minutes. On Monday and Wednesday we started with announcements and questions. Tuesday and Thursday meetings began with acknowledgements and apologies, which quickly became a favorite ritual. Only one agenda item was discussed at each meeting with the goal of reaching consensus or a majority decision. Rather than having the leader call on people during the discussion, I asked students to call on each other to speak. The system improved considerably when the group decided to require girls to call on boys and vice versa. Deliberations became more focused, and more voices were heard.

One discussion was about the perceived inequality of my expectations for student work. After a lesson with a small group, I often posted follow-up work we agreed upon, listing the participants' names. Because I assembled small groups in so many different ways, the overall perception was that some students had to do more work than others. The group decided that everyone should have an equal number of assignments (their word), if not the very same ones. They voted on three assignments I should make each week and expect every student to do them all.

It was not a good time to explain what I thought about individual pathways and self-directed activity. I was glad they were discussing work so seriously. It appeared they knew why they came to school each day and cared about everyone learning. For me there was no choice—make three assignments each week for everyone, and stop posting activities after small group lessons.

Quickly I discovered that if the three assignments were broad, every student could accomplish them in a way suited to their abilities and readiness. The first posting of three assignments read: "Multiply, sentence analysis, plant story." Multiplication fit easily into each person's math program, and everyone had been in lessons about sentence analysis at some level. After posting the list, I pointed out a seldom-used box of plant stories on the botany shelf and suggested a matching game with the pictures, labels, and stories. A small group was soon gathered on the floor, spreading out the pictures to play the game.

Most had other ideas for a plant story. Carl went online, found the name of an exotic plant he had heard about, and wrote a report about it before the morning was over. Piper and a friend wrote poems about plants, and others wrote fictional accounts of plants that talked and had plant adventures. This variation caught Carl's attention, so he began working on a second response to the assignment:

Episode 1

Suddenly the Great Spider plant strangled the evil Thanksgiving Cactus! Then the giant T-Rex jumped out of the Venus fly trap and started marching towards the Spider plant. But Spider plant side-kicked Grape vine and Grape vine shot grapes at T-Rex. But it was too late. The Fly trap had eaten Spider plant. But Spider plant tickled it until Venus opened her trap. Spider plant jumped out to find Cactus parachuting down to the rescue!

The three assignments for the second week specified reading twenty poems, perimeter work, and adjectives. Again, everyone seemed able to define for themselves the appropriate level of challenge. The readers made long lists of adjectives found in their books. Some students worked with the neglected adjective grammar box. A few seemed unsure what adjectives were, so we gathered together and used article, adjective, and noun cards to compose adjective phrases, both serious and silly. Later I noticed others playing the same game, completing an assignment.

Students whose self-directed projects already guided their daily activities regarded the assignments as filler, although occasionally one launched a new exploration. For students struggling to manage their time, the three assignments provided a gateway to productive work. In conferences, they were often eager to show me how they had completed the assignments. The weekly three-assignment format persisted with considerable success throughout the school year, and the group took pride in having resolved the problem.

Another agenda item we tackled in a class meeting was respect for the "teacher's pet." Several classroom jobs rotated daily, the most important of which was being the leader, also known as the teacher's pet. The leader lined up the class, led them to activities like gym or lunch, and delivered the mail at the end of the day. There had been numerous complaints about people failing to cooperate with the leader. We had even received two complaints from other teachers about the conduct of the class in the hallway, which seemed to be either the fault of the leaders or students in the line. The problem was discussed in a class meeting and recorded in the minutes:

> We discussed respect for the teacher's pet. The problem written on the agenda said people are yelling at them, but the teacher's pet is doing what they think is right. Liam said sometimes the teacher's pet uses their authority to do favors for their friends. Ellie said sometimes they say: You're not

the boss of me. Javier agreed people talk back, like saying—No, YOU be quiet. Lydia said people talk at the end of the line. Friends go back there and keep talking when they are sent back. Carl asked why not just be responsible and separate yourselves from people you would probably talk to. Piper said mostly our problem is going to lunch. Maybe we should have assigned places in the lunch line next to people who don't talk to you. Liam made a motion that we line up in alphabetical order when we are going to lunch or recess. Quyen seconded the motion. We voted. 12 people voted for the motion, 7 opposed it, and there were 2 abstentions, so the motion passed.

The discussion suggests broader participation and developing confidence in the group's ability to solve problems. Daily meetings did not continue past November, but the frequent meetings built respect for the process and improved skills. Weekly meetings held in subsequent months continued to be more orderly and usually productive.

Geometry caught fire in our midst when Bella and Liam discovered the tiling game. With some of the younger students, I had reviewed the plane figures in the geometry cabinet, introduced parts of the polygon, and demonstrated how to use a ruler and a sharp pencil to trace them. They began tracing the figures accurately and soon began combining polygons to make imaginative drawings. When we gathered to share work, I passed around a crosscut piece of honeycomb, pointing out its hexagonal pattern.

Within minutes after the group disbanded, Bella was filling a large sheet of paper with adjacent hexagons. She brought the encyclopedia volume B to my table and began reading to me all about beehive communities. Gradually she filled her hexagons with drawings representing special beehive cells—one for the queen and her eggs, one for the nursery, and others for the workers. The page became a complex study of both geometric shape and the workings of a beehive. Her design drew attention, and soon other students were experimenting with the hexagon pattern using a variety of color designs, a few as beehives.

Then Liam tried covering a page with pentagons and discovered a different pattern. It didn't cover the page perfectly but yielded an interesting shape at regular intervals. Experiments with other polygons revealed surprising new patterns. Within two weeks we had an entire wall covered with arresting variations on the tiling game.

A feeling of community was in the air. Building on the group's enthusiasm, I introduced my favorite Thanksgiving project, a geometry construction called A-Cute Turkey. I repeated the lesson quite a few times until every student successfully made at least one—if not five—A-Cute Turkeys. The project requires work with a compass and a protractor, a first experience with both tools for many. Some practice exercises are recommended before the turkey work begins. The A-Cute Turkey's body is a large circle and the head a much smaller adjacent one. From the center of the larger circle, lines drawn to the rear of the turkey create an array of adjacent acute angles. Curved lines connecting the periphery make closed angles shaped like feathers. Measuring each acute angle comes next. Then the magic of colored pencils can turn A-Cute Turkey into a superhero or a pirate or pilgrim. The project introduced a new set of shared skills and opportunities for mutual admiration.

November 16th journal entry:

Today I made an acute turkey named flyer. He is mostly cool colors. I made him have a propeller hat and I made it flying in the sky.

—Carl

On Tuesday before the Thanksgiving holiday, we took a bus downtown for a Colorado Symphony concert entitled *Musica Latina*, a program planned especially for students. We had spent several afternoons the week before listening to a CD of the music we would hear (sent by the symphony) and learning about the composers Ginastera and Reveultas and Villa-Lobos. Each student made a small book with a page for each piece, writing the name of the composition and the composer at the top and then drawing an artistic interpretation of it while listening to the music. Occasionally I danced through the middle of the room to dramatize the mood of the music, like the stirring themes of Arturo Marquez's "Danzon."

Everyone entered the grand concert hall eager to hear

the music played live. With each new piece, the students' emotional engagement appeared to increase. The music was as thrilling as expected.

Back at school we shared thoughts about the concert. I suggested everyone write something about their experience on the last page of their book—what they liked best, new instruments they heard. Some students added pictures of the instruments while others enhanced their original drawings.

And then someone requested that we listen to the CD again. I resisted a little while, thinking perhaps we should just treasure the echoes of the live music, but others joined in to insist they wanted to hear the music again—and there was time before dismissal. So I started the CD. Everyone listened intently to the first two compositions, and then "Danzon" began. After the first few bars, Piper and Bella and Javier were on their feet dancing to the music. They were joined slowly by one student after another, some dancing hand in hand, others forming a circle, until finally everyone was on their feet dancing as one—some with arms stretched high to join hands, a few couples breaking off, everyone smiling and laughing. It was a celebration of music, dance, and friendship. The community hummed.

5 December
The Mirror

Holding up the mirror is not about reflecting how student behavior is pleasing to us, but reflecting the student as a person so she can be pleased with herself.

—Howard Glasser and Tom Grove[1]

December always brings grammar and geometry to my mind. Adding Montessori grammar symbols to the poetry of the season reveals delightful word patterns. A holiday tree decorated with geometric ornaments creates a surprising "geome-tree."

We were at the end of first semester, so this was also a month to evaluate progress. Before looking back, however, I proposed planning a holiday program for families with songs and poetry and plenty of decorations. The response was enthusiastic.

Everyone had been reading poetry because of the previous assignment, so I asked them to begin thinking about a favorite poem they would like to study and learn. I also assembled a small group of the oldest students to plan the tree. Lydia, Maya, Liam, and Blake worked well together, deciding to cut out three equilateral triangles of graduated sizes and mount them on the bulletin board above the library. They calculated the area of each triangle and wrote their calculations conspicuously on the tree parts. The project made quite a commotion, stirring everyone's interest.

When the tree was completed, I gathered younger students for a lesson about lines of symmetry, showing them how to find the lines by carefully folding precut polygons. The children dotted the lines of symmetry with white pencils to reveal interesting interior shapes. Decorations were added with colored pencils, glitter, and glue, resulting in pretty ornaments for the tree. When it was full, the polygons became snowflakes falling around the tree, which Bella named our "symme-tree." I put the photo of the earth from space on the top.

The other students were now eager to contribute, and most were also ready to work with the area of rectangles and squares. After a review lesson, they got busy with graph paper, making packages to tack up under the tree, each decorated with the calculations for its area—and a bow. The packages reminded the tree makers about the area of quadrilaterals, and they added more gifts to the pile. Soon the younger students were making packages and calculating area too. And everyone was finding lines of symmetry to make more ornaments, enough to adorn the bulletin board and the windows and the doors. The room shimmered with anticipation.

I had brought in an autoharp and taught several students how to accompany some holiday songs requiring just a few chords. Isabella learned how to play them quickly and taught Camilla. Soon they were teaching others. One of the first songs we sang with the autoharp was "O Christmas Tree." On a Friday afternoon, when the tree on the bulletin board was fully decorated, someone suggested we change the beginning words to sing "O geome-tree, o geome-tree, how lovely are your branches." Pairs took turns on the autoharp while we practiced the new lyrics.

We were also planning for a poetry recitation. In the classroom library we had all the Shel Silverstein books as well as those of Jack Prelutsky, Robert Frost, Christina Rossetti, and Langston Hughes. When I assigned reading twenty poems, students had discovered other poets in the school library, and I added a few collections from the local library. One afternoon we listened to Silverstein reading some of his poems. Several afternoons concluded with children reading their favorite poems.

For the program I asked everyone to choose one poem they liked enough to study, copy, illustrate, and memorize it. The first December assignments included copying the chosen poem carefully, leaving enough space above each line for the Montessori grammar symbols. To help them remember the symbols and their predictable groupings, we began several mornings symbolizing lines of "'Twas the Night before Christmas" together. (See appendix E.)

When students began drawing the symbols above each word in their poem, they discovered patterns. Some poets repeated the same grammatical structure many times, some used a preponderance of verbs, and others clearly delighted in adjectives. Most of the children were also able to identify rhyming schemes and meter. When they finished the symbolizing work, I suggested creating a graphic for displaying their poems.

I had been working through the poetry project myself, choosing a poem about the moon. Now it fit nicely on two pages, which I pasted onto a silver crescent. With some added glitter, my simple example was enough to inspire many imaginative displays for the poems.

To my utter amazement, Hayden followed the poetry work through all of its stages, finishing with a four-foot drawing of a giraffe whose skin design on its neck was the string of letters in a Silverstein poem, mimicking his illustration. Would Hayden actually be able to stand up in front of an audience to recite his poem? With permission, I hung his giraffe prominently on the wall, hoping he could rise to the occasion. Ronnie, Destiny, and Alma chose very short poems but seemed intent on following the project each step of the way.

As the date for the program drew nearer, the challenge was memorizing the poem, but most were surprised at how easy that was after all their prior work. Soon we had daily recitations. Almost everyone was eager to take a turn standing, announcing their poem and poet, and reciting the poem for classmates. Most seemed ready and eager to meet their public.

The program was scheduled for the last full day of school before the holidays. Lydia and Isabella designed an invitation we could reproduce. Everyone personalized the fliers for parents, grandparents, aunts, and uncles. Someone suggested refreshments; others volunteered to bring them. I looked for the holiday tablecloth. Another suggestion was inviting the class across the hall to be our first audience before the main event. I made the arrangements.

The students had other ideas for the program. I had taught a Hanukkah dance I thought would be a good opening, but they agreed the Japanese fan dance would be more fun and a much better beginning. The first song would be "O Geome-tree" to celebrate the decorations. After the poetry recitation, we would finish with the folk song "This Little Light of Mine." It was a favorite because the many verses provided as many opportunities for different accompanists on the autoharp, one student holding the chords down and the other one strumming. I suggested sitting in a single long line so all would face the audience. That gave them another idea. The two students in the middle would stand for the first verse, and additional students on each side would stand as the song progressed until everyone was on their feet for the last verse about the universe.

My most important job, they insisted, would be to sit in the middle of the first row and prompt them if they forgot their poems. I was happy to comply. It was the perfect place to appreciate them one by one. Like a mirror, I could reflect back the confidence and competence I saw as each child took center stage.

Guiding students through self-evaluation activities was another opportunity to help students see their best selves. Being a mirror means first taking time and concentrating energy to find in every child what is valuable and special. The second part is reflecting back to them exactly what you see so that each affirms his or her own worthiness. By guiding the children through a careful process of studying their best work, I hoped each would recognize and appreciate how much they had accomplished during the semester.

One morning I handed everyone a list of their scores on math-facts tests, fifteen-minute tests they took at the end of each month. The tests aimed at increasing the number of correct facts one could calculate in the allotted time. Those who could speed through two hundred problems in the four operations could add to their scores by solving multiplication combinations for the elevens, twelves, and fifteens.

Almost everyone had five scores from tests taken August through December. I coached them through the steps of constructing line graphs, plotting their scores, and connecting the dots. The resulting lines ascended as expected for most. A few ragged lines suggested lapsed efforts or bad days, perhaps immersion in other pursuits. I asked everyone to write a few sentences telling the story of the line on their graph.

Another step in the self-evaluation process was reviewing work the students had chosen for inclusion in their portfolios. At the end of each month, I asked students to review their work and choose the best samples in four categories: best writing, best use of language, best art, and best math. The most challenging part of this exercise was taking time to look at everything they had done during the month. Each student had an individual folder in the filing cabinet where I placed work they had given to me. In addition, they had writing samples in their daily journals, drawings in their animal-classification folders, and projects on poster boards. I encouraged them to clean out their desks in the process, an activity that often uncovered lost papers or unfinished projects.

When students decided on their best work samples, they brought them to me for review. We agreed on their choices, and then they wrote a cover sheet giving reasons for choosing each sample. In a brief second meeting, I read their comments and placed the assembled collection of best work in the portfolio. All the loose papers went home, the first dispersal accompanied by a letter explaining to parents that the student's best work had been archived.

When the December work samples had been chosen, I gave everyone their portfolios and asked them to find all the handwriting samples they had chosen from August through December. Then I posed several questions to help them think about what progress might look like: Had the size of their writing changed? Were they using more capital letters? Were more words written on the line properly? What changes did they notice? I asked them to describe what they observed about their writing progress in a short paragraph, which I later included in the semester-end progress reports.

I would have liked to continue with evaluations of math work or art, but their patience had expired.

On the afternoon before the last day of school, we staged the dress rehearsal. Everyone helped carry the tables into the hallway and arranged chairs to form two long rows with a performance space in between. When the class next door arrived and was seated, the students danced their way into the room. Javier made a welcome speech, and then the poetry recitation began. I sat in the middle of the first row with all their poems in my lap. Few needed prompting that afternoon, and none needed help when they performed for their families the following day.

And they all came—parents and grandparents, uncles and aunts, with siblings and cousins crowded on the floor in front of their elders. After the opening dance and welcome speech, I briefly explained the symbolized poetry displayed on the walls and the geome-tree. Then I took my place on the front row, cradling the poems and reflecting back smiles that revealed happiness experienced only when giving your best.

Twenty-five poems, including Hayden's giraffe poem, were recited, almost without error. Boys and girls used eye contact to alternately call on one another so that the presentation was nearly seamless. At the conclusion of the recitations, the applause was long and heartfelt. The choreography for "This Little Light of Mine" went as planned, and then everyone joined in singing "We Wish You a Merry Christmas."

We had added an additional long row of chairs for the family audience, but the performance space in the middle of the classroom was still vacant, creating a perfect corridor for the Virginia reel. I hit the play button for some bluegrass music, and the dance began. Mothers with sons, sisters with younger siblings, grandmothers with grandchildren— all danced together in celebration of the children's success and the happy occasion we were sharing with our extended community. It was difficult to bring the dancing to a close, even though refreshments were waiting.

I remembered a Japanese teacher telling me the most important thing was to make happy memories so that children would always want to come back to school. As I watched my students dancing with family and friends, I saw memories in the making. Perhaps even their parents and grandparents might want to come back to school again.

We exchanged holiday wishes as the children departed with family or mounted the school bus steps. Two full weeks of separation lay ahead.

6 January
The Psychologist

To find the interpretation of children's desires we must study them scientifically, for their desires are often unconscious. They are the inner cry of life.

—Maria Montessori[1]

On the first day back, Lydia arrived with a pile of letters and stuffed the mailbox—a letter for everyone. The mood of the children seemed amicable but guarded. Some chatted about movies they had seen. Horror, sci-fi, and romance films were recalled in short exclamations that suggested a limited grasp of the plots. When we gathered, Carl described his trip to visit relatives in Missouri, and Blake told us about living in his dad's yurt, snowshoeing every day. Ronnie described his two new video games, which reminded others of their new telephones and iPods. They were eager to bring them to school, so we scheduled a sharing afternoon for Friday. Many showed up with new electronic devices, but they proved difficult to share and were quickly abandoned when someone brought out their new game of Twister. New sets of magic markers were popular too.

I didn't come with plans for that first school day in January. It seemed important to hang back and observe closely, to look for growth and change. To be honest, my daily planning was minimal. I usually came to school with a general idea of how the day would progress, especially if I expected to present a lesson for the whole class. For years I planned lessons in advance for small groups and individuals but was often frustrated with the results. When I gave the lessons as planned, I was forever breaking up the extended work period I meant to protect. In the last several years, I had gained the confidence to make spontaneous judgments about lessons. At the end of each day, I recorded those I had actually given.

Quite a few students resumed work easily that first day after the long holiday. Martin pulled out all the boxes of beads and began building the decanomial again. Liam, who had discovered Rick Riordan's *Percy Jackson* series, gathered his personal book club together to share the find. Javier got busy drawing the interior of the planes that took his family to Puerto Rico and back.

As I sat quietly watching from my table, several children stopped by to confide life-changing events. Isabella's parents decided to get married, and she had been an attendant in the wedding. A new baby was expected. Piper's mom couldn't make the January mortgage payment, her third month of default, so Piper and her mom had been packing up all their belongings with plans to move in with her grandma. Bella reported that her mom, pregnant again and moving in with her boyfriend, was taking only the youngest baby girl with her to the new place. Bella and her two brothers would be staying where they were, living with an aunt and a grandmother. Mom had promised Bella she could ride the school bus sometimes and stay with her at the new apartment.

Each personal revelation reminded me of Montessori's equation of intelligence and the "I" factor that represents the constantly changing internal life of the individual. The students who confided in me had been profoundly changed. They would need special attention and empathy. I thanked Piper warmly and publicly when she showed up with a big box of things she saved for the class while clearing out their house, including a talking globe that required lots of batteries. Every day I asked Bella about her plans after school. Together we lived for those days when she could ride the bus and be with her mom.

Despite his successful participation in the December poetry program, Hayden appeared to have regressed. Once again we had to evacuate the room when he had a temper tantrum. During the autumn months, Hayden's mother had often spent mornings in the classroom trying to persuade him to do the work she saw others doing. When she stopped coming because of a new job, a series of meetings with the estranged parents and the special education team determined that Hayden needed more academic support. Subsequently he left the classroom about six hours a week to spend time with the special education teacher. Her reports indicated that he was able to concentrate on reading and writing activities in her room, where there were only two or three others working under her supervision. He was usually calm when he returned to the classroom but still participated only in animal classification and an occasional class meeting. When the special educators attempted to assess his reading skills at the end of the semester, he once again refused to cooperate.

There were more meetings in January with more people involved to discuss Hayden. Specialists from the district attended and recommended a program of behavioral modification. It began with promised rewards for compliance and consequences for noncompliance to get Hayden "on track." A special educator from the district was assigned to oversee this program one-on-one with Hayden in the classroom several mornings a week. Following her instructions, I created a small poster board with pictures of typical work activities in the classroom, each with a Velcro strip on the back so that Hayden could move the options around to plan his day. He was instructed to choose two pictures of "required" work for thirty minutes at the beginning of the day before choosing a third activity, which could be work he really wanted to do.

The program made no sense to me, especially in light of Dr. Montessori's observations of children's work cycles. When she meticulously graphed work choices of individual children over extended periods, she found they usually chose several easier tasks before they engaged in challenging work. I had seen this pattern repeated many times in my classrooms. In a letter to Hayden's team, I made an effort to explain my concerns about their proposed interventions:

> The fundamental pedagogical principle that anchors Montessori education is following the child. In my experience, that is easier with younger children— the younger they are, the clearer their purposes. Hayden is only in the second grade. Given his strong

personality, I don't think we have a choice anyway. I will try to help him conform to classroom norms. Regarding his academic work, I will continue suggesting new projects to engage his keen intellect. However, my goal is to help students find meaningful work they have chosen for themselves.

Hayden's compliance with the new system was minimal despite its various props and punishments. He developed a range of resistance strategies, frustrating his special helper and winning most of the battles that involved her stern directives and time in the hallway. I tried to maintain the distance of a scientist, observing closely without interfering. What frustrated him the most? When was he able to engage in meaningful work? Was our classroom a good place for him? What is best for students who exhibit special needs? How does their behavior affect other students?

Two former classes came to mind. One was a lower elementary class with a good balance of first-, second-, and third-grade students. Michelle was one of the oldest in the group, a nine-year-old who was socially and academically more like a seven-year-old with severe physical disabilities. The oldest girls, third graders, took turns helping her change her diaper several times a day. Her language was difficult to understand, but she was always included in discussions or games. When the class decided to put on a rendition of *Annie* at the end of the year, they all agreed Michelle should be Annie. From very early in the year, that class functioned as a true community. They all treated each other as best friends.

Years later there was an autistic girl named Laurel in one

of my upper elementary classes. Early in her fourth-grade year, she was befriended by one of the more accomplished girls her age. Soon Laurel was accepted and included by everyone—for the entire three years that she remained in the class. The classroom climate grew increasingly inclusive and benevolent during those years, and the students' ability to work together seemed unusual.

I wondered what my students might learn from Hayden and how they could support him. One day, when he was out of the classroom, I gathered everyone together to enlist their help. Most were aware of his problems and seemed glad to air their frustrations. Then they made suggestions about how they might help him. In the following days, I observed many students deliberately making efforts to follow up on their own suggestions. Martin invited him to do an experiment in magnetism, and together they explored the classroom for two days in search of magnetic objects. Later they built a needle compass together.

One morning someone invited Hayden to work together at the puzzle table, but the district helper insisted he "save that for later," which completely shut down his engagement. He continued to challenge all the specialists' plans for his rehabilitation, but his interactions with his classmates began changing. He ceased having tantrums and participated more often with the group, who had become more patient with him.

Maya's attitude was still a problem. She often flirted with the youngest boys, who mostly ignored her. Her social experiments extended to group activities such as class meetings, refusing to join the circle but sitting nearby to whisper cryptic remarks. When we met to review her work, she continued resisting new math lessons and returned to her single desk to multiply or make notes about flying squirrels. She was increasingly rude and uncooperative with all adults. A meeting with her father seemed to make matters worse.

Evelyn and Destiny were still mutually reinforcing work resistance. In an effort to improve their self-esteem, I had made them class representatives for a school-wide philanthropic project called the Penny Harvest. They attended the weekly meetings during the first semester and reported enthusiastically about the project at class meetings. I hoped they would return after the holiday break with a new sense of belonging and an eagerness to work. However, Evelyn's older sister, who lived with Evelyn and her mother, had given birth to a second baby over the holidays. Destiny's mother had a new boyfriend, a good-looking young man who sometimes picked Destiny up early in the middle of the afternoon. The apparent progress toward assimilation I observed at the end of the first semester had disappeared.

Reading journals helped me understand the children's predicaments. Everyone kept track of daily work in their journals but also wrote to reflect, suggest, react, and complain. Mornings began with journal-writing. Often I provided a thought for the day, a famous quote or a short poem I asked students to copy and illustrate. Sometimes I wrote a word on the board for a dictionary study. Other times I asked students to write personal reflections—what they had done before coming to school that morning or what worried them. I also reserved about ten minutes at the end of both morning and afternoon work periods for reflective writing. When it seemed difficult, I encouraged students to write a few adjectives or draw a picture. Most began writing simply about their school experience and also about problems at home. Sometimes they drew cartoons to express strong feelings. Journals were private. I was the only person allowed to read what they wrote.

I tried to read half the journals at the end of each week and write a short response in each. When I detected trouble, I often read the child's journal after school. Sometimes I could identify gaps in understanding and think of a lesson to resolve confusion. "Pychologizing" the curriculum was Dewey's expression for the process of figuring out how to connect the student with the right curricular experience. Often journal entries hinted at personal problems, suggesting the need for a private conversation, mediation between peers, or a discussion in a class meeting. The beginning of the second semester seemed overloaded with stressful changes both inside and outside the classroom.

Fortunately, Martin Luther King Jr. was born in the middle of January. His birthday provided a good reason to return to important themes—caring, cooperation, taking responsibility, serving others. I posted one of Dr. King's quotations to start several mornings. We spent two afternoons reading a play about his life.[2] I taught several easy civil rights songs: "We Shall Not Be Moved," "I'm So Glad," "We Shall Overcome." We slipped the songs into appropriate places in the script and assigned parts to volunteers after the first reading. On the second day, a few students showed up with costumes, and in the afternoon we performed the play for ourselves.

Before adjourning for the holiday weekend, we had a conversation about justice, equality, and the responsibility of everyone to make a contribution. In Dr. King's words, "Anyone can be great because everyone can serve."

"Thank you, Dr. King, for making it so I could have all my black friends. And for helping to make peace," wrote Carl.

When we reassembled after the long weekend, I told the story of math, which I called the History of 1-2-3. My first prop was a smooth hand-sized piece of granite. I made a series of charcoal marks on it—one, two, and then three horizontal lines. Next we examined pictures of cuneiform on ancient tablets with similar strokes and a wedge-shaped tool like one that might have made those marks in clay. Using the later cuneiform style, I drew symbols for the number 123 in base system 60. When I progressed to the Egyptian pictographs for numbers 1, 10, 100 and 1,000, I noticed several older students copying my drawings in their journals. Together we figured out how to write the composite number 123 in hieroglyphics.

I moved on to a story of Hindu merchants on the Silk Road, perhaps the first people to make use of the empty set. I had prepared a rectangular pan half-full of damp sand and a tool I made from a short dowel to make parallel grooves in the sand. As I told a story about selling silk buds, I described how the merchants' accounting clerks might have kept track of sales. I counted loose, colorful beads into the first groove, stopping at nine and exchanging them for one bead placed in the next groove, resulting in an empty set— our zero. Lancelot Hogben's book *The Wonderful World of Mathematics*[3] provides good details for the story.

My audience was rapt. I had told the story many times to older students who usually pretended disinterest, but this group was down on the floor with me, making new numbers with the beads in the sand and remarking on the genius of it. Someone pointed out the similarity between the grooves in the sand and the wires on the abacus we used in the classroom. We placed beads carefully in the grooves to show the number 123.

Next we wrote 123 with the Greek's alphabetical numerals and then with Roman numerals, a system already familiar to some. Together we solved a multiplication problem the Roman way, laughing at the complicated process and remarking on the efficiency of the decimal system. As I concluded the story, I encouraged students to practice counting in a different number system. Some began right away using adding machine tape, already a favorite tool used for counting multiples.

Responses to stories are unpredictable. Next morning Destiny appeared at my table with the checkerboard in hand, asking for a lesson on multiplication, which I had suggested more than once. We began with the very first exercises, reading large numbers and recognizing the powers of ten located in colored diagonal rows on the checkerboard. She found it difficult but stayed at my table for most of the next two days to work with it. On the third morning she took the checkerboard to her own table and taught Evelyn how to compose and read large numbers. Together they appeared to be grasping number hierarchies and multiplication. Perhaps the doors of intellectual curiosity were opening.

t was time for our field trip to the Museum of Natural History. In late autumn I had introduced the Timeline of Life with some of evolution's highlights—the dominance and decline of trilobites, the corals and sea lilies taking calcium into their skeletons to clean up the oceans, the first plants creeping onto land to pave the way for the first amphibians, the great dinosaur era with its mysterious ending. The timeline had been on display for a month, and some had studied it closely. Liam wrote a report about giant cephalopods and drew a life-sized example for the hallway wall. On the afternoon before our museum trip, I read aloud Virginia Lee Burton's marvelous book *Life Story: The Story of Life on Our Earth from Its Beginning up to Now.*[4]

At the museum we spent most of the morning wandering slowly through the Hall of Life, a series of dioramas depicting the progression of prehistoric eras. The largest display was the Hall of Reptiles, complete with a two-story skeleton of Tyrannosaurus rex. Students spread out to marvel at the gigantic remains, and some stopped to read the descriptive markers. I stood quietly next to Evelyn, who was trying her best to read about the curved-neck dinosaur whose skeleton was stretched out before her at least twenty feet long. When she got stuck, I helped her finish reading the text. After a pause, she looked straight at me. I could see the light behind her eyes as she exclaimed, "You could do a report about long-necked dinosaurs! I'm gonna do that when we get back. I'm going to write a report about long-necked dinosaurs!"

In *Montessori: The Science Behind the Genius*, author

Angeline Stoll Lillard explains Montessori's emphasis on the importance of the freedom to choose. She writes, "Learning to make good choices for oneself is considered part of one's education…thus, even if choices might be difficult to make, learning to make them is seen as part of Montessori education."[5]

For Evelyn, that act of resolve, of choosing something on her own, occurred halfway through the school year, but for her it was the beginning. We were scarcely in the door before she began hunting for books about dinosaurs. She invited Destiny to help her find facts and write notes.

Hayden located an illustrated book about early reptiles and began building a three-dimensional paper montage of the dinosaur era. Maya was the first to admire it. She was devoting herself to multiplication with many zeroes. Isabella was collecting notes about Dr. King. Bella announced plans to write a report on plants. Piper decided to duplicate the Timeline of Life. Determined at first to do it by herself, she soon grasped the enormity of the undertaking and accepted Ronnie as her first assistant. Soon others were helping.

On a morning in late January, I looked out over the class and saw everyone engaged in their work. I couldn't resist playing a reprise of "Just Remember That You're Standing on a Planet That's Evolving." A few hummed along.

Montessori Guide to Psychological Observation

Work

Note...

- when a child begins to occupy himself for any length of time upon a task.
- what the task is and how long he continues working at it (slowness in completing it and repetition of the same exercise.)
- his individual peculiarities in applying himself to particular tasks.
- to what tasks he applies himself during the same day, and with how much perseverance.
- if he has periods of spontaneous industry, and for how many days these periods continue.
- how he manifests a desire to progress.
- what tasks he chooses in their sequence, working at them steadily.
- persistence in a task in spite of stimuli in his environment which would tend to distract attention.
- if after deliberate interruption he resumes the task from which his attention was distracted.

Conduct

Note...

- the state of order or disorder in the acts of the child.

- his disorderly actions.
- if changes of behavior take place during the development of the phenomena of work.
- whether during the establishment of ordered actions there are: cries of joy; intervals of serenity; manifestations of affection.
- the part the child takes in the development of his companions.[6]

7 February
The Tour Guide

Snow is falling
A beautiful sight
Snow is falling
It plays with the light
Snow is falling
It plays its game
Snow is falling
It makes all that's different look the same!

—Our Class

Children stood at the windows to watch the snow fall. Winter temperatures often meant indoor recess when students were free to return to work after lunch, and many did. Others played games or made up skits like "hitchhiker." Although Montessori programs often skip traditional midday recess, our school district required it every day for everyone. An afternoon game of kickball, drawing outdoors, or trips to the garden did not count.

Dr. Montessori emphasized the importance of excursions beyond the classroom for elementary students. Going out into the community provides access to broader resources, opportunities for service, and freedom with responsibility for students. The first trips might be visits to other classrooms and then explorations around the building. Eventually students can plan excursions to local businesses, libraries, or museums to pursue their interests. Elementary children, she wrote, need "to establish social relationships in a larger society. The closed school, as it is conceived today, can no longer be sufficient for them."[1]

Like many city schools, ours was located in a slightly depressed residential area. The closest library was two miles away. The streets were not safe for children to walk independently to the few stores nearby even if such a trip was allowed. When several former students had become engaged in plant classification, I encouraged them to plan a trip to the botanic gardens across town. It turned into a huge project, requiring two parent drivers, lots of advance paperwork, and a substitute because a teacher had to go along. District policy even required two additional adults for a class walk to the local park.

In private schools where I taught, regular camping trips had provided a rich extension of the classroom. Hiking, sleeping in a tent with friends, and cooking breakfast over a fire you built yourself are experiences that expand horizons and build personal confidence. Our public school district had an excellent outdoor education site—six hundred acres in the foothills of the Rocky Mountains furnished with cabins, a dining hall, and classes supervised by a talented staff. On my first hike there, I had been astonished when the children exclaimed over spotting a squirrel. They lived in the shadow of the Rockies but seldom left their city neighborhoods. Unfortunately, camping at the district's facility was reserved for fifth graders, so that wasn't an option for this group.

We were still entitled to one bus for a field trip. Improvements in our class meetings suggested the children might be interested in seeing democratic lawmakers in action. I knew the state legislature would be in session throughout the spring months at the capitol, a historic building downtown. It seemed like the perfect place for our next excursion.

When I called the transportation office, however, they informed me there were no busses available until April. Most dates in March were blocked because of the statewide tests. I reserved the first available date in April, but I knew that was too long a wait for another adventure. I would have to conduct an in-house tour.

Because it was Black History Month, we were reading *Leon's Story*[2] together. A generous parent bought enough books so that each student would have a copy, and we were concluding afternoons reading the book aloud. It tells the story of the boyhood of Leon Walter Tillage, who grew up black in the Jim Crow South. The coauthor, Susan L. Roth, heard him talk about his background at a school assembly where her son was a student and Leon had long been the custodian. She subsequently met with him and transcribed his memories, then added abstract illustrations to produce a powerful book for intermediate readers. Because the text is written in Leon's vernacular, the vocabulary was manageable for everyone in the class. They grew increasingly eager to take turns reading aloud, and almost everyone participated in the discussions. Many children found events in *Leon's Story* simply unbelievable, similar to their incredulity about Dr. King's childhood and segregated classrooms.

Maybe a tour of African history would help them understand. It would begin with the story of early humans. I had two illustrated timelines and *Human Origins,*[3] Richard Leakey's book for young people describing discoveries his team made in the Olduvai Basin. The photographs are excellent. I was ready to conduct the tour.

One morning I stood at the farthest side of the room and described four million-year-old footprints, a nine-foot-long trail made by two hominids at a place called Laetoli in Tanzania. Taking several steps toward the middle of the room, I told the story of Lucy, whose skeleton suggests that around three million years ago, a three-foot-tall female with arthritic legs wandered the Olduvai plain.

The next day I introduced the first Timeline of Humans, which depicts tool-making, fire-building, and migrations. The lesson unfolded as a series of questions and suppositions. What distinguished humans? Was it fire or perhaps the discovery of using fire to cook? What kinds of words did early humans find most useful and why? What kinds of tools did they make first? Why did humans wander northward, eastward, and westward, crossing narrow land bridges until human groups lived on every continent?

The discussion suggested experiments about tools and early technologies. Next morning I invited everyone to experiment with wedges, the inclined plane, and other simple machines. In the art center, I provided a heap of leather scraps with tools for pounding and cutting and piercing. Everyone seemed to remember how to conduct themselves through a morning of experimenting. The activities were punctuated with occasional exclamations.

"Humans can make tools because their hands are free. The first tools were rocks like the wedge. Other tools are: battery, spoon, and fulcrum," wrote Carl.

A few days later we studied the second Timeline of Humans together. At its beginning are pictograms of animals and human figures etched or painted on cave walls during the Upper Paleolithic Era. One line drawing depicts three hunters with spears on the left side of the picture and only two deer on the right, perhaps an example of early subtraction. The second half of the timeline shows long horizontal lines increasing in height to suggest rising temperatures on earth and the subsequent leap into new human enterprises—weavers and pyramid builders and the Trojan War.

After the discussion, several children explored the folders about ancient civilizations and displayed some of the pictures in front of the timeline: Sumerian writing and hieroglyphs, pyramids and temples, early Greek pottery. Carl, who had written a report about Norway, began collecting notes about the Vikings. Piper invited Cloe to help her finish a report about King Tut, paving the way for a tour of Africa's ancient kingdoms.

As I prepared to be the storyteller again, I was reminded of Dr. Montessori's remarks about teaching history: "The story of the past can be just a boring account of events. It must not be given that way. It must be given like a fairy tale. The stories must be short, with a few well-drawn characters; the environment must be limited, unusual, and very clear. They must all be built around something fantastic."[4]

Equipped with a map showing locations of the first African kingdoms and a set of posters depicting the great kings, I told their stories. I began with the story of Akhenaton's City of Dreams and his beautiful Queen Nefertiti. There was Taharqa, king of Nubia, who led his armies against the invading Assyrians when he was just sixteen years old. Hannibal, ruler of Carthage, crossed the Alps with his elephants to battle the Romans. Mansa Kankan Mussa, king of Mali, led 72,000 people from Timbuktu to Mecca and back. Askia Muhammed Toure, king of Songhay, divided his country into provinces with governors and judges. Afonso I, king of Kongo, developed the first school system in Africa. Shaka, king of the Zulus, used weapons and tools with such cunning that he built the Zulu tribe into a powerful nation of more than a million. Menelek II, king of kings of Abyssinia, merged several kingdoms and resisted European colonization.

Now the kings paraded across the long display counter. Students gathered around to examine the pictures and stories written about each one on the poster. In the school library, Blake found a book that told the whole story of Mansa Musa.[5] I read it aloud to the class.

And then, in the midst of our African tour, the United States and its NATO allies launched a military intervention to support the rebel forces fighting Libya's Colonel Muammar al-Qaddafi of Libya. The fervor of Tunisia's revolution was spreading across northern Africa. Rebel forces were also taking up arms in Bahrain and Yemen. In the news coverage that followed, I found an article in the *New York Times* by Graham Bowley explaining how the northern African region had been an embattled crossroads for centuries. The article began with a description of Hannibal's campaign and the sacking of Carthage, now Tunis. The illustrations included an old serigraph of Hannibal's army attacking the Roman troops at the Battle of Zama, where the Carthaginian army was crushed. It also had a map showing current hot spots of the region—Zama, Tunis, Algiers, Tripoli, Benghazi in Libya, and El Alamein in Egypt. When I brought the newspaper to school, a crowd gathered to examine the details. Our tour of ancient Africa had collided with current events.

Quickly I introduced a second map of Africa to show how ancient kingdoms had been overwhelmed by European colonization. The color-coded map showed how the continent had been divided up by the British, French, Dutch, Spanish, Italians, and Belgians. Briefly I explained how the conquerors had created borders and named new countries, disrupted ancient cultures, and dismantled the work of the great kings.

A few days later I introduced a current map of Africa showing many of the colonized countries with new African names. Our tour was speeding through centuries of history to catch up with the new chapter of African history being written.

We were on a world tour now. I began posting newspaper clips about the Arab spring on the world map and connected news clips to countries with red yarn. One morning I posted a picture of Mohamed Bouazizi and told the story of his courage in Tunisia. Students brought other clips portraying new acts of revolution and courageous defiance.

They also brought pictures of spring earthquakes and floods. One morning Carl brought his school picture and suggested posting it on Norway, his ancestral home. Others remembered they had families or ancestors from other countries and posted their school pictures on the appropriate countries.

Students often gathered in front of the map to discuss new posts. Listening to their conversations indicated some confusion about the relationships of countries, so I began reserving the end of the day for discussions about world events. I gave everyone a black-line map outlining all the countries, some quite tiny but each large enough to contain a number. On notebook paper attached to the maps students made lists of the countries they identified and numbered. When we discussed a country, we often composed a sentence about it they could write next to the country's name. Many wrote their own favorite facts. The mapmaking discussions lasted only a few weeks, but several children continued adding new countries to their lists throughout the spring. Piper eventually had more than one hundred countries on her list.

As the Arab Spring unfolded on our bulletin board, we often talked about the reasons for revolution, the causes of the unrest, and why people would risk their lives to defy their governments. The students were surprised that many countries still had kings and alarmed at the number of dictators.

It was time to go downtown and visit the capitol of Colorado, time to see how government in our own country worked.

But first, there were those statewide tests threatening to derail our tour. How could I help my kids sustain their excitement and stay engaged?

8 March
The Advocate

*Knowledge can be best given where there is eagerness
to learn, so this is the period when the seed of everything can be sown, the child's mind being like a fertile
field, ready to receive what will germinate into culture.
But if neglected during this period, or frustrated in its
vital needs, the mind of the child becomes artificially
dulled, henceforth to resist imparted knowledge.*

—Maria Montessori^{1}

Nearly a century ago Montessori decried
test results, calling them useless and
misleading. She believed that asking students to apply
abstract concepts before they were fully formed compromised concept formation. Often she compared teaching
to the sowing of seeds, especially in the elementary years,
when students' imaginations provide rich and fertile soil
for new seeds to sprout, take root, and grow. Testing for
understanding too soon is like pulling up newly sprouting
seeds to check on their progress. Anyone who has done that
knows what happens.

In 2002 Colorado began requiring all public elementary

schools to administer the Colorado Student Assessment Program, widely referred to as the CSAP. Originated in conjunction with the federal No Child Left Behind legislation, the test was designed to measure how well students were learning content specified by the Colorado Model Content Standards. For a decade Colorado schools administered the test, although it was revised several times. Each new edition involved new item construction and field testing followed by publication of new test booklets and test preparation workbooks for every level, an egregious and regrettable waste of resources.

Only one grade level could be tested in the same room, but the classes at our school included multiple grade levels, so scheduling the CSAP tests was difficult. The result was the total disruption of the regular school day for everyone—for three weeks.

In his book *The Case Against Standardized Testing* (2000), Alfie Kohn recommended setting aside the regular curriculum for two or three weeks before testing in order to help students understand test format and quirky questions. I took his advice and began meeting small groups at the end of February to help them prepare.

Kohn also suggested sending a letter to parents explaining the need to set aside the regular curriculum for the purpose of test preparation. If parents expressed dismay over diminished time for learning, he suggested furnishing them with the names and addresses of local school board members.

I knew it would not be acceptable to express my strong objections, but I did write parents a letter before testing began to explain how the tests would disrupt our daily routines. I suggested those disruptions would probably upset the children and affect their behavior at home in unexpected ways, requiring extra patience and understanding. Also I described the alternative teaching methods I would be using to help students get ready for the tests. And I did mention they could write school board members if they wanted to express their objections.

One year I had attended several long meetings with district personnel to advocate exempting Montessori students from testing based on our educational theory and practice. Despite thoughtful responses and apparent agreement with me on many points, the group clearly regarded such an exemption impossible.

Now I simply did my best to prepare the children for the testing formats and procedures. I had seen items on CSAP tests for years and knew what kinds of computation and word problems third and fourth graders would encounter. Graphs of all kinds, for example, were ubiquitous on the math tests along with measures of central tendency. I brought out the boxes of trinkets to review bar graphs, including how to find the median and the mode. Most remembered making a line graph of their math scores at the end of the first semester, and a few had made line graphs of temperatures over a month's time, data they found on a weather website. They had presented their graphs for the class, talking about mean temperatures and average rainfall. We revisited the graphs students had made to describe class characteristics early in the year as well as the survey results Destiny and friends had presented.

To this day I cannot figure out why the mode, median, and mean have taken on such importance for fourth graders. Similarly, many of the terms and concepts found on the reading and writing tests constructed for elementary students seemed arbitrary. We discussed sample test questions about literature, but the answers were often puzzling. As one group tried to detect the answers to questions about a short paragraph they had read, Piper looked at me in all seriousness and asked: "I'm just curious. Are there right answers for these?"

Ah, the plague of right answers. They were seldom a primary goal in our classroom. Even in math, discussing whether answers were reasonable was often a better way to advance understanding than simply checking for correctness. Now, however, it seemed important to help students connect probable math questions to concepts developing with Montessori materials. I reluctantly taught some computation shortcuts, precluding discoveries individuals were about to make on their own.

As the testing weeks approached, I worried. What would happen to Ronnie's growing confidence with fractions? Destiny and Evelyn were both reading more and better every day, but not on grade level. How would the word tasks and comprehension questions affect them? Would Blake find a place to show his grasp of geometry? Would Bella's incisive reasoning skills shine through? How would the tests affect my second-language learners who were slowly gaining courage with the English language? And Hayden? He would be tested individually as a special needs student, given extra time and support, but I doubted he would cooperate and was sure the tests would damage his self-esteem. Montessori's metaphor of pulling up new seedlings by their roots often came to mind.

When the testing began, I resumed group work we had temporarily suspended. Between sessions we often discussed world affairs, adding a few more countries to our lists. Some gaps between testing sessions were long enough for animal classification. We had worked through all the invertebrate phyla during the first semester and moved on to classes of vertebrates. During the testing weeks, I introduced a new order of birds every day. Writing definitions and drawing seemed to provide the mental rest students needed. The familiar work became a highlight of each day.

Some mornings we began with warm-up exercises. Students took turns demonstrating favorite stretches and stunts, a way of relieving the tension before tests. After morning tests we often held a short class meeting where frustrations were expressed about the test schedule and missing gym, which happened frequently. At the end of the day we sang songs, read poetry aloud, or danced. We began learning a dance to "Pata Pata," a South African song Miriam Makeba made popular calling for resistance to apartheid. Both the song and dance have a quality of defiance that provided for some physical expression of frustration.

I was amazed at the students' resiliency and proud of their efforts to do their best. Most seemed to simply accept tests as part of school life. I continued encouraging them, assuring them, thanking them for good attitudes, and making occasional speeches about the limited significance of the tests.

Throughout the first decade of standards-based testing in Colorado, numerous reports summarized the results. There were internal district reports and newspaper stories analyzing the reports. Hardly ever was there a statistically significant result—neither an improvement nor a decline in the scores. There were always a few changes in the aggregated data, but no trends sustained over time

This problem of statistics without significance came to mind when I read the results of a 2012 study comparing "top educational systems" worldwide. Results released by the National Center for Education Statistics reported that "American fourth graders are performing better than they were four years ago in math and reading, but students four years older show no such progress." The report concluded that students in the United States perform better than the global average in all subject areas—except for students from poorer schools.

What are we to make of such reports? How could they possibly contribute to good decision-making about funding or instruction?

T he last week of testing was reserved for makeups, which would take various students out of the room for unpredictable periods. It wouldn't be an easy week, and then there would be spring break.

I sat down to make a plan for rescue and recovery. Planning seems most important when keen interests begin to fade or a major disruption has occurred, like testing. It was time to reflect on students' recent experience and consider new themes to explore. In my archives, I found the following mix of reflections, possibilities, and plans:

March 20—One week before the break.

Spring! Tomorrow present the geography chart about revolution and rotation and the seasons. Act it out! ALSO use the two words as a "double word study" first thing Monday morning.

NOTE: They keep improving on this exercise for studying a word—finding it in the dictionary, learning what kind of word it is, writing their own definition, drawing an illustration. They are learning habits of mind, how to think about something.

HELP them find half-finished reports and aim for Friday presentations of at least a few: ground squirrels, Utah, Mars, Alphabet History, Maine, Tunisia, Lincoln.

What about biography next? The Lincoln report would be a good model if it is finished AND we all read *Leon's Story* AND we still haven't heard Piper's report about George Washington. Learn to write an outline for a biography—good topic for seeing the utility and simplicity of outlines. Generate it together and encourage taking simpler, shorter notes.

ART: Get Mrs. Vance to teach us how to draw someone's face.

HOMEWORK this week: Ask two adults to name people they admire and wish they knew more about! Friday before Spring Break post the lists and we can start getting ideas for biographies we would like to write!

MATH: Start up some good geometry this week. Use Insets of Equivalence and get some equivalence designs going. Older ones can start doing proofs— start with triangle = rectangle.

New kinds of SENTENCE CONSTRUCTION might revive us too. Colorful fun with language. Remember patterns we love that were missing from the tests.

The teacher is a weaver, starting new patterns, adding a wild colorful thread here and there, unexpectedly. Inviting students to create something beautiful out of what they think and learn together.

REMIND everyone to finish their Aves pages this week! Mammals coming up.

9 April
The Ringmaster

A companion characteristic to the children's interest in morality and justice is their tendency to worship heroes. They have an intense interest and admiration for great men and women who have pushed to the limits of human capabilities.

—Paula Polk Lillard[1]

There was brisk chatter about famous people and personal heroes when we came back together after spring break. Bella found her envelope of notes about Mansa Musa in her desk, and Javier located his research on the Wright Brothers. Within two days, almost everyone, including Maya, Destiny, and Evelyn, had chosen someone for the biography project. We gathered to brainstorm an outline. Then there were many trips to the library, *World Book* volumes all over the place, note cards constantly in short supply. Each student launched the project with apparent confidence, everyone except Hayden.

Not surprisingly, he seemed to have suffered more than the others during the lost month of March. His participation was marginal again, his attitude negative. I suggested drawing a portrait of someone he admired.

Encouraged by the welcome buzz of engaged workers, I gathered a few older students together to introduce binomial squaring. They had all constructed consecutive and non-consecutive squares with bead bars and bead squares, and they had learned to write the binomial in both numeric and algebraic terms.

The new lesson aimed at squaring numbers (from 11–99) using the peg board and pegs—green for units, blue for tens, and red for hundreds. Together we constructed the square of 2 with four green pegs and then worked our way up, building consecutive squares by adding unit pegs along two sides until we had the square of 14, a very large square of 196 green pegs. I then introduced the work of exchanging: ten unit pegs for one blue peg and ten blue pegs for one red.

By working first down each row of green pegs and then across from left to right, we turned a large square of unit pegs into a much smaller one composed of one red in the upper left corner, two blue rectangles extending across the top and along one side, and a square of green pegs in the lower right corner. Immediately the students recognized the familiar arrangement of squares and rectangles, and someone commented that it was a much better way to represent the number 196. I showed the simplest way to calculate the sum from the array of pegs (100 + 40 + 40 + 16.) Most everyone nodded and seemed to understand.

As the lesson concluded, I encouraged them to repeat the work with a partner, but I detected a lack of confidence. Next morning Martin and Javier went back to calculating bead square binomials with rubber bands. No one tackled the new work on the peg board.

F inally it was time for our field trip to the capitol. The day before the trip, someone brought in a newspaper article describing plans to restore the deteriorating gold leaf on the dome. We were ready to see it up close.

When we arrived, we were surprised to find the lawmakers all standing around outside the building. There had been an emergency evacuation. I corralled my group in one corner of the spacious lawn to wait, but several older students asked if they could wander over to shake hands with the legislators. They came back with big smiles. Fortunately, within fifteen minutes everyone started drifting back into the building.

Knowing it would take time to get the lawmaking business up and running again, I led the class up to the history museum on the top floor and then farther up a narrow staircase, where we could walk around an interior balcony directly underneath the gold dome. We saw the scaffolding for the gilding project, and the view of the city was spectacular.

Then we headed down the stairs to the floor where the galleries overlooking the lawmaking assemblies were located and took seats in the house gallery just in time to see the assembly called to order. When the speaker rapped the gavel, we all jumped a few inches out of our seats. We convened our class meetings with a small gavel, but that official rap gave our replica new significance. Next there was a reading—was it the minutes or one of the required readings of a bill to be discussed? It was difficult to understand any words but clear that the reader had been formally trained in speed reading.

The speaker thanked the reader and then called for announcements. A queue of legislators quickly formed at the side of the podium. A few announced committee meetings, but most came to the podium asking to be excused from the afternoon session, explaining their reasons at some length. One legislator asked to be excused from the next day's sessions. With each request, the house members were asked to give their assent. Finally there was another rap of the gavel, and recess was declared until one thirty. We hadn't witnessed lawmaking debate, but everyone was amused by the litany of excuses and totally approved of a long midday recess.

Next we walked across the central part of the capitol to the gallery above the senate chamber. There legislators had also recessed until the afternoon. It was an opportunity to move around the gallery and discuss what we saw below—comfortable high-backed rocking chairs for each senator, large containers of candies on the long front counter, desks littered with Starbucks cups, computers, papers, and more candy. (There was a lot to like about democracy!) Above the chamber were beautiful stained-glass windows picturing outstanding men and women in Colorado history. I pointed out a few.

As we gazed down at the lawmaking arena of democracy, I thought about the presentation Carl had made about the Vikings. He had drawn a four-foot-tall illustration of the Viking world depicted as a giant tree. In the upper branches, Carl explained, lived the gods who directed human affairs. The trunk of the tree and the activity around it represented the life of the people, and the roots below contained the underworld where evil was lodged and bad memories were stored. What a contrast! Here we were sitting in the treetops—the citizens at the highest level, the elected officials sitting in the chamber below to make laws in accordance with the people's wishes. What would we find below?

We descended the many staircases, stopping on each floor to see what was happening. On the next floor down the legislative chambers emptied onto a circular balcony filled with the hubbub of conversations between legislators and lobbyists. The next staircase took us to the main floor, where we visited the governor's office and the office of our representative, who took a few minutes to welcome us. Then we headed down to the basement, where we had snacks alongside lawmakers who were deep in conversations over their sandwiches and coffee. We finished the morning with stops at some of the Colorado history exhibits and had lunch on the grounds outside, enjoying fine weather and spectacular views of our city from atop the capitol's hill. Looking up, we could see workmen on the scaffolding around the dome, which clearly needed new gold leaf.

Back at school, we discussed the trip at length. As we talked, the children made notes or drew pictures in their journals to capture their favorite memories of the trip. They were still sharing observations and asking good questions when the afternoon came to an end. I passed out souvenirs I'd been given and sent them off to share the adventure with their families.

Next morning I couldn't resist comparing the Viking world with democracy. I retrieved Carl's illustration of the Viking world from the hallway display and posted it beside the chalkboard, pointing out the arrangement of power it represented—gods in the treetops, people living in middle earth, and the underworld below. Next to it I sketched an outline of the state capitol. Under the dome I drew the galleries with stick figure people sitting where we sat the day before. Below I drew a platform for law-makers and, below that, the doorway to the office of the governor. Democracy turned the Viking world upside down.

And then Liam had another idea. He came to the chalkboard and drew a different tree with the word *dictator* written up among the top branches. Below he wrote "Family and rich friends," and around the trunk he drew lots of people. Someone suggested putting some rebels plotting to overthrow the dictator underground among the roots.

There was a long silence. Almost everyone was drawing something in their journals, thinking their own thoughts.

Gradually everyone drifted off to other work. Some went back to collecting notes for the biography project. Jared, one of only three African American students in the class now, switched his biography choice to Barney Ford, a Coloradan pictured on one of the stained-glass windows of the senate chamber. Ford was instrumental in the movement to free slaves in Colorado and later to extend voting rights to African American men.

Bella was back in the kitchen, taking care of plants she had started from seed following her extensive report on plants. Several students were finishing drawings of birds. Someone was back at the art table finishing a leather pouch. Maya was working on very large multiplication problems, and Destiny was sitting close by her, moving beads around on the checkerboard. Hayden was on the floor, counting the cube chain of seven, arranging all the squares in the correct locations. Lunch came too soon. The morning ended when it seemed the momentum of self-directed activity was at its peak.

What the students needed from me now was unencumbered time. My job was to step aside, and in doing so, I found a new calling as the ringmaster. I helped students find spaces to work that would not disrupt other activities. I directed attention to peer presentations. I reveled in the simultaneous activities transpiring in a single room and directed the attention of visitors so they could see past the apparent chaos to enjoy the show too. My mother, who taught fourth grade for many years, had visited my classroom one morning and was only able to watch a few minutes before asking, somewhat anxiously, "What are all these children doing? It looks like a circus in here!"

There was still an empty ring where I wished more mathematicians were performing. One morning I invited the fourth graders back to review the lesson on the binomial square. As we worked through another problem transforming a square of green pegs into the hierarchical pattern, the students started to work ahead of me. They were remembering how to do it and discussing the parts as they built the binomial. When it was completed, several wanted to continue, carrying the materials to the floor to start another problem.

Next morning they were at it again, and someone had borrowed a second peg board from the class next door. Now two groups were on the floor transforming big green squares into binomials. By midafternoon Bella was closely observing one of the groups. She asked if she could join and invited a few friends. Soon we were submerged in shared discovery learning. Peg boards and pegs had been borrowed from all over to sustain multiple projects. I helped find space for all the activity surging around me, but my part in this performance was strictly outside the ring.

When most students had completed their biographies, the sharing began. There were lively question-and-answer periods after each presentation and much admiration for the portrait work. I hung a gallery of their drawings in the hallway—Mansa Musa, George Washington, Abraham Lincoln, Martin Luther King Jr., Rosa Parks, John Muir, Maria Montessori, Jackie Robinson, the Wright Brothers, Susan B. Anthony, Amelia Earhart, Eleanor Roosevelt, Barney Ford. Alongside the portraits I posted Ralph Waldo Emerson's words: "There is, properly, no history; only biography."[2]

Writing autobiographies seemed like a natural follow-up to the biography work and a good way to conclude the year. And so in the month's last homework folder I included a questionnaire about the particulars of each person's birth—place and time, parents and siblings, and special events of babyhood.

April concluded with a rush to complete unfinished projects. The experiments with tools for cutting and piercing leather had generated products students decided to contribute to the market for Cinco de Mayo, a much-loved celebration at the school. There was some scrambling to complete unfinished bookmarks and pouches and bracelets. Under Bella's direction, a number of students began painting small flower pots in anticipation of Mother's Day. The rush of year-end events on the school calendar—Cinco de Mayo and field day and orchestra concerts—were being announced regularly at class meetings. We were headed for the finale, anticipating the final acts.

10 May
The Student

Our one duty is to learn from him on the spot—and to serve him as best we can. Thus we must first become excellent observers of him. What the child shows is right, inasmuch as it provides us with a guide to reality, to the truth.

—Maria Montessori[1]

Elementary children are fascinated by the story of their own birth and babyhood. With information gathered from family members about the beginning of their lives, they went right to work on the first chapter of their autobiographies. Some had birth certificates in hand, and others brought photos. The writing process seemed to come easily for almost everyone. Hayden drew a picture of himself as a baby and attached the questionnaire with his parents' answers written in his own handwriting.

Homework each week included questions for subsequent chapters of the autobiographies. Students interviewed family, friends, and sometimes former teachers to find out about their childhood and earlier school life. On Fridays homework folders with surveys completed were arriving, and Mondays were for starting new chapters—Childhood, First School, Early Grades, This Year, My Future. Occasionally we gathered to share favorite memories about best friends, vacations, or injuries.

Some of these stories had already been told during birthday celebrations. When parents were able to come for a birthday, they would arrive at the end of the day, usually with cupcakes. After our special birthday song, the parents shared anecdotes and answered questions about past injuries (the more serious the better) or most embarrassing moments, as well as favorite childhood foods and first words. Now new information and surprising stories were turning up. I learned many things about the children I wish I had known earlier.

Writing a new chapter for autobiographies was one of the three class assignments each week in May. The project helped stabilize classroom work amidst the excitement of the many special events and interruptions on the calendar.

One morning I tried introducing the next step in binomial squaring, a shortcut with more advanced notation, but the students I invited went right back to the familiar steps of the squaring work many were still enjoying.

More successful was an introduction to the Big Bank Game, which begins by laying out an array of number cards, units to millions, to calculate the products of very large multiplication problems. I played the game with a small group, gathering six students almost at random. It works best when two students act as bankers, two as customers, and two as accountants, all taking very specific roles on the way to finding a solution. The group caught on quickly, and within the week they had taught half the class how to play. There were almost always six people at the bank game table, and sometimes Destiny and Evelyn were in the mix. Everyone was learning something different about multiplication. What I learned, for the umpteenth time, was that children learn best from each other.

Throughout the year I photographed students at work or on special occasions. I had the pictures printed often and displayed them in a photo album to create a class history book. For young students in January, September seems like the remote past. By May the year's events in pictures constitute true history. Browsing the album was a favorite pastime.

Now I invited everyone to choose a few pictures from the album to illustrate the chapter of their autobiography about "this year." Some chose one of the photos for the cover, and others used their official class picture. All had original ideas for their covers.

It was also time for each student to assemble the many pages of their animal-classification work and make a cover for that book, too. We had studied two orders of mammals at each meeting in April and May, and their drawings of mammals were increasingly accurate. For the cover, I suggested drawing a favorite animal and listing its classification. A cheetah would be identified as follows:

Kingdom: Animalia
Phyla: Vertebrata
Class: Mammalia
Order: Carnivora
Common name: Cheetah

With Animal Classification written above the drawing and the listing below, the cover provided a culminating lesson about classifying animals. Then came perhaps the most important step—the organization of the many pages they had created. Which pages belonged to the invertebrate group? What was the order of development in the classes of vertebrates? I helped each child assemble their pages, remarking on wonderful drawings and improved handwriting. Some discovered that pages were missing and set about creating them. Several others insisted on redoing some of their early pages when they realized how much better they could have done. I preferred the originals. When all the pages were in order and the cover was ready, they assembled their books with colored plastic loops. Everyone, including Hayden and Ronnie, made a book.

Another project near completion was the Adopt-a-Tree work. Homework assignments for the project had been collected in special green folders, which now held numerous drawings and observations and tree samples. Kathryn had made sure students who didn't do homework had regular trips around the school to observe their adopted trees. In mid-May I asked everyone to make a final observation. Many of the trees had blossomed, and some had new cones. Samples came in with final notes and drawings. I made a few suggestions about assembling the observations and drawings into a booklet, but most students proceeded confidently, doing it their own way. Some were inspired by the developmental sequence in their observations and wrote a story about the tree's life. Piper wrote a tree poem. Javier included a list of all the animals he had observed in and around his tree. Destiny created a beautiful cover with blossoms that had fallen from hers.

As the end of school drew near, we spent a morning working on portfolios. Almost everyone chose their auto-biography as their best writing or best use of language or best art in May. Then I asked students to read essays they had written in January describing their goals for the second semester. To decide how well they had met those goals, I suggested looking at the work samples they had chosen for their portfolios since then. Several children began making a line graph of all their math test scores for the year.

For those who looked uncertain about comparing goals and work, I proposed choosing one goal and looking at work samples to find evidence of improvement. I also asked them to read the chapter in their autobiography about the current school year. It was challenging work, but quite a few children began writing about their progress. When several agreed to share their reflections, there was further page-turning through portfolios, more writing, and more readings. The shuffling and sharing continued for almost an hour. Then I asked what they hoped to learn next year. There were some thoughtful answers. A few named books they were definitely going to read, and many said they were going to do lots more squaring. The portfolios went home the last day of school with their final report cards tucked inside.

There was still a short week remaining before school's end—just enough time to put on a play. After they had worked on portfolios all morning, I distributed scripts in the afternoon for a short play called *Pushing Up the Sky*.[2] The prospect of a performance seemed to revive everyone.

For our first reading, I assigned some speaking parts, but there were many choral responses so that everyone could participate in the read-through. We talked about the story and then read it again with different volunteers in the speaking parts. We also discussed possible scenery and costumes. The afternoon ended with a flurry of creative invitations to our theatrical offering the last afternoon of the last full school day of the year.

Over the long weekend I set up two stage flats made for previous productions in the classroom. Simply built wooden frames covered with strong canvas, each flat was made of two 4 × 8 panels hinged so that it could be free-standing. The two units (four panels in all) created the backdrop and also a backstage space when positioned slightly away from the wall. I covered each of the panels with blue paper to suggest the sky.

Several students arrived after Memorial Day with sketches for scenery. They gathered to study each other's drawings. When we met as a group, it was quickly decided we could use parts of everyone's ideas, but Maya would first sketch a big picture on the flats. Then she would ask others to add more detailed drawings.

Next was the issue of costumes. Since almost all the characters would be dressed as members of the same Native American tribe, we decided everyone could assemble their own costumes. Having just presented her project on the history of clothing, Lydia volunteered to be the costume mistress and help those who seemed confused or insisted they had nothing appropriate to wear. Next I defined props. Every character needed to secure a long pole, and a few more props had to be made. I described the job of stage manager, the person who would keep track of props and organize everything backstage. Liam volunteered for the job but insisted he wanted to be an actor too.

After a break, we gathered to read the play again. When I began asking for volunteers to play certain roles, I found they had already agreed amongst themselves who should take which roles. Ronnie and Hayden would be the two small animals that came on stage at the beginning of the second act, and Bella would be the little girl who had the speaking role because she was the shortest girl. The tallest girls and boys in the class would be the chiefs. Carl and Piper both wanted special parts, so I made them the narrators. We met later to divide the narration into equal parts.

Everyone seemed satisfied with their part and left the circle with a purpose. Small groups formed to read the script together. Several students conferred with Maya and went to work drawing mountains across half the backdrop. Another team cut long strips of brown paper that became logs for a house on the other two panels. A small group met with Lydia to talk about costumes. The high level of focus was impressive.

In the afternoon, I kept my suggestions to a minimum as they collectively blocked the three short scenes. Liam organized everyone backstage so they were all hidden but could easily come onstage from the correct side. Luckily most of the characters were on stage most of the time. We walked through the play several times, talked about learning cues as well as lines and how to anticipate an entrance. Hayden and Ronnie decided to be a dog and a rabbit, but they were so engaged in acting their parts that it was difficult to get them onstage at the appropriate time. Nevertheless, we had a play by the end of the afternoon. We concluded by sharing ideas for a musical opening and suggestions for songs at the end of the play. Someone volunteered to bring plastic stars for the ceiling, which would shine after the lights were off, a perfect special effect for the ending.

There is no group activity like a theatrical performance to bring people together as a team. Parts of everyone's sketch for the scenery were eventually included, and every student who wanted to help draw or cut or paste participated. The job of costume mistress turned out to be more challenging than expected when numerous children told Lydia they couldn't find anything at home like the costumes we had discussed. The crisis was brief, however. The next day she brought in a few extra blankets and wraps. Several children brought in poles of different kinds, enough to provide for all the characters. Hayden and Ronnie spent a great deal of time making masks with ears and whiskers that wouldn't fall off when they jumped around on all fours. Carl worked for several hours covering the cardboard backing for his script with Native American designs.

The students organized themselves to practice a musical introduction with rhythms played on maracas made from different-sized plastic bottles, which produced different tones. They had made the maracas with the help of a high school student who visited the class several times in April to give music appreciation lessons. The group also practiced a song we had sung many times about rivers, forests, and mountains, which seemed a fitting conclusion for the show.

On Thursday morning we invited the class next door to see our official dress rehearsal. It was sketchy but entertaining. The animals only appeared for the final song.

For the afternoon performance, we emptied the classroom of all the tables and asked the custodian for extra chairs, expecting a crowd. We were not disappointed. The special educators showed up with a few students, and so did the principal. Siblings in the school arrived and were seated on the floor. In the rows of chairs behind them were parents and grandparents, uncles and aunts. There was a full house.

The play opened with a surprisingly musical performance of songs played on the homemade maracas, and then the students quietly took their places backstage. Piper began the show by declaiming the opening narration by heart. Characters said lines like they meant it; everyone's costume stayed on their shoulders properly; and at the end of the second act, the dog and the rabbit entered stage left on cue. When the players came onto the stage to take their bows and sing their last song together, we all sat amazed. They had worked together like a well-oiled machine to present a remarkably moving story without an embarrassing moment. Their faces shone, telling us their rewards were as great as our pride.

I don't remember the last morning of the school year very well. We must have brought the furniture back into the classroom. We probably cleaned out our desks and put everyone's individual stack of belongings into plastic bags with the portfolio on top. We probably gathered to sing songs, and I believe we danced the "Pata Pata." I am sure we all flooded out into the hall to dance the "Macarena" with other classes, a traditional way of ending the school year on the second floor. I'm sure we cried and hugged and that many of the youngest students were surprised the school year was over.

I wondered what the summer meant for them. Some would surely be signed up for soccer or basketball camp, and maybe someone would be on a swim team. But most would spend countless hours watching TV or playing Nintendo, safe activities in a big city. Their grandparents, aunts, and uncles would look after them and their younger siblings. It gave me some comfort to know they would be able to come to our school during the summer for free breakfast and lunch. But saying good-bye was tough for me. Each one of the students had shared their story with me, and I had learned so much.

11 June
The Reflective Practitioner

If the child has the freedom to develop at this age, the result will be seen at the adult stage.

—Maria Montessori[1]

D r. Montessori's assertion that results of developmental education will be seen in adulthood is a cautionary note for a culture preoccupied with immediate gratification and measurable outcomes. But her message is clear: look for results of your work with children in their adult lives. If we return to the metaphor of teaching as planting seeds, it is useful to think of apple seeds and how long they must grow before producing trees and apples. And we must ask, "What kind of adults do we hope our children will become?"

This is a question I like to raise in community meetings with parents. I ask them to talk in small groups about their goals for the children and then to share their conclusions. The qualities they list are almost always the same: self-confidence, kindness, generosity, honesty, gratefulness, patience, happiness, loyalty, motivation, fulfillment in work, courage, perseverance, interest, creativity, self-discipline. No list ever includes "intelligent" or even "college-graduated."

The parents' priorities are remarkably similar to the goals of education Montessori reiterated many times. We will know we are achieving our goals, she said, when we observe children developing perseverance, gentleness, affection, politeness, serenity, patience, flexibility, equilibrium, the capacity for abstraction, a strong will, and spontaneous creation. Again and again Montessori returned to perseverance as a true indicator of internal development. Recent studies of success in higher education support her assertion, finding that the personal quality of perseverance is a better predictor of college success than academic achievement in high school.

In a Montessori setting there are no year-end test scores, no class standings, not even pass or fail grades by which to measure students' growth. Moreover, the qualities we deem important are extremely difficult to measure. How can we evaluate our success in promoting students' development?

As I sifted through the pile of class documents and farewell notes I had received the last day of school, I found the final issue of *Dragon's Blood*, a twice-yearly school publication of student work selected from all classes. Often someone would ask permission to dash downstairs and put a poem or drawing in the collection box, and several children in the class had been thrilled to find their work in the midyear edition. There hadn't been time on that last day for me to peruse the year-end edition. Now when I did, it fell open to this poem by Maya (age ten):

MATH

I love to do math
Math is my favorite thing to do
In my classroom

I love all kinds of math
Like multiplication and division
What I like of those two
Math things to do
$12 \times 11 = 132$
And $100 \div 10 = 10$
Those are my favorites

I love math so much
That it makes me think of playing sports
And taking a vacation.

A full-page illustration for her poem was printed on the next page.

All year I worried about Maya's attitude towards math and her fear of the multiplication tables. Her poem made the outcomes plain. She learned to multiply successfully with large numbers, she memorized the facts of multiplication and division, and she understood division as a reciprocal function of multiplication. Best of all, she fell in love with mathematics, giving it high rank alongside sports and vacations.

Then I found a poem by Bella (age eight):

MARY CASSATT!

O Mary Cassatt!
Is the water so hot?
The tub is for feet,
And the girl is so sweet.
Your water looks real.
The mother is still.
The girl is so tanned,
And the mom holds her hand.
Your painting is loved,
And I love your stuff.

Throughout the year Bella had inspired me with her initiative. She was an exemplar of self-directed work and peer coaching. One of the youngest students in the class, Bella's influence alone was a testament to the benefits of mixed ages in a class, no matter which three years were combined. She benefitted from working with older students too. Her mathematical reasoning leaped forward when she learned squaring and the big bank game from them. She was a constant writer—of stories, letters, reports, songs, and poems. Her Cassatt poem suggests writing might have helped her cope with the emotional stress she had experienced during the year.

Under the *Dragon's Blood* issue I found Carl's gift to me, the cardboard backing of his script, which he had covered with beautiful Native American designs. Reflecting on Carl's body of work over the year, I could only take credit for setting him free. With the slightest hint of a new direction from me, he always took off at high speed and created something unique. With Carl, I was often the learner. His progress was unquestionable, his path of development truly his own.

What about the development of all the others? In the pile was my official lesson plan book, which held a record of lessons I had given and to whom. I also had lists of projects students had presented, the poems they had memorized, and books they had read in literature study groups. The portfolios containing their best work had gone home. I often shared student work archived in portfolios with parents during conferences, but found they preferred familiar evidence of good work. Spelling scores, facts test scores, and weekly assignment checklists met that need, so I kept them rigorously. When I examined the assignment checklists, I noticed almost all students had completed most assignments. However, facts tests, spelling scores, and completed assignments are hardly the stuff by which to measure personal growth.

I also wondered how I could evaluate my success as storyteller, companion, guide, community organizer, mirror, scientific observer, advocate, ringmaster, and student? The most important work of the adult in the classroom, Montessori had emphasized, was studying the students and promoting a social medium in which subject matter intersected with experience to encourage growth. To what extent had my roles promoted growth?

The Native American play during the final week of school suggested a learning intersection of interest, effort, cooperation, and individual growth. It showcased a community characterized by mutual respect and genuine affection, a group able to set a goal, work together to make it happen, and celebrate reaching their goal. Perhaps my role as community organizer had helped to promote the sense of community they projected. I thought of all their faces shining with pride at the end of a program put together by a winning team. As ringmaster, I had drawn their attention to all the marvelous activity taking place in the classroom, helping them appreciate one another's efforts. And as a mirror, I had reflected back to each one their unique worthiness. I think I saw new pride in their eyes during the curtain call.

Remembering the students all sprawled out on the floor, working together to turn big green squares of units into binomial squares or playing the big bank game, I was convinced most of the children finished the year feeling more confident as learners. When I recalled their increasing composure as they stood before classmates to share their stories, poems, and reports, I felt sure most had increased their ability to speak effectively, to value their own ideas, and to believe their ideas had value to others. I hoped my role as companion, psychologist, and advocate on their behalf had helped build their self-confidence.

n *Spontaneous Activity in Education,*[2] Dr.
Montessori provided a list of behaviors
indicative of an evolving internal order, that mysterious
inner sanctum of the human brain. She suggested looking
for fixed attention, persistence, patience, repetition, the
polarization of the attention, spontaneous creation, and
joyful obedience.

The capacity to fix attention varied widely among
the students. Carl, Quyen, Liam, and Piper were almost
always able to move forward with their decisions and fix
their attention quickly on whatever they chose. Hayden's
attention was often so fixed on his pursuits that there was
no way to introduce another activity, a characteristic of
attention often associated with younger children. Many
others improved their ability to sustain fixed attention as
they became more confident directing their own projects.
Writing autobiographies appeared to focus everyone's
attention.

Whenever I observed the class, I saw evidence of persistence that often outlasted my observation time. One day
I watched two girls carefully sort their notes about prairie
dogs into piles all over the middle of the classroom floor, an
activity that took all morning. On two occasions Martin and
friends spent two days systematically exchanging bead bar
sets to build the tower of cubes. When Ellie returned from
her special education sessions, she often spent the rest of
the morning solving a division problem with three divisor
boards. Destiny and Evelyn first experienced perseverance
with their mixtures experiments and found it again when
they began writing reports and multiplying on the checkerboard. Many children had difficulty beginning projects

but were able to persist once the work had begun. Others seemed to self-direct so consistently that persistence was a natural state of being.

Persistence is associated with repetition, which sustains and enhances polarized attention. When students drew polygon designs for a week or calculated area to pile up presents under the geome-tree or squared the binomial repeatedly, I saw the amazing results of polarized attention. When they created beehives out of hexagons, giraffes out of poetry, and pouches out of leather scraps, I saw spontaneous creation. When five of the six bank game players slowed down to explain once again how you exchange ten ten thousands for a hundred thousand, I was impressed by their patience. And when everyone obeyed Liam's instructions to be quiet for ten minutes backstage, I was astonished. I think that was joyful obedience.

Recalling parents' descriptions of the kind of people they hoped their children would be provided another set of scales for measuring success. Had students become more self-confident, kind, generous, honest, grateful, patient, happy, loyal, motivated, courageous, interested, and self-disciplined?

Hayden's next teacher reported that he was reading and working on grade level and getting along well with others. I have to call that amazing, a testament to his inner resources. Bella continued to motivate others with her confidence, her wellspring of multiple interests, and her generosity. Camilla enrolled in a middle school highly regarded for its science and technology curriculum. Her parents reported that she was discovering new interests, mostly in books. Carl went directly into an upper elementary class where he was the youngest and smallest, but his self-confidence was unwavering. Maya started the following year at another school but soon returned to finish her Montessori career and became a leader of the sixth grade girls. When I chatted with Javier a year later, he told me he was helping in a primary class, reading with younger children and teaching them about airplanes.

Reports about Destiny the next year were not good. She had caused social turmoil in her new class and was struggling academically. I am convinced having the same teacher for three years would have significantly improved her chances for success. Evelyn and Ronnie both left the school for unknown parts. The stories do not all have happy endings.

Because the qualities we hope to see in our students develop over such a long period of time, we adults who travel with them briefly must be resigned to knowing little about the effects of our efforts. However, the Montessori community would benefit immensely from longitudinal studies of our graduates. We know about many distinguished people like the founders of Google, Amazon, and Wikipedia who have Montessori backgrounds. There are surely many more success stories to uncover—inventors, good citizens, entrepreneurs, humanitarians, and leaders in all fields who have been deeply influenced by their experiences in Montessori classrooms.

Although it is difficult to discern a student's growth on the scales of personal qualities, sometimes parents or teachers send back encouraging reports. Katie was a former student who struggled with mathematics but worked diligently with every Montessori material and presented a fine project about the history of Florida when she completed the upper elementary class. She was everyone's friend. She continued on to a public middle school in seventh grade. At the end of the first semester, her homeroom teacher called me to report that Katie had won the Good Citizenship Award and to thank me. She described Katie as one of the kindest, friendliest, and most generous students she had ever met. But she said the most important quality Katie had brought to her class was the courage to ask questions. When she didn't understand something, she raised her hand and asked for help. The teacher assured me middle school students seldom do that, but Katie was so well liked that others began asking questions too, which significantly changed the learning climate. That kind of feedback suggests the quality of outcomes we hope for.

I look forward each May to graduation announcements and the pictures that follow. My former students are often wearing honor garb showing their academic success. There are many reports of leadership awards. When George received the Good Citizenship Award upon his graduation from middle school, his mother graciously took time to thank me:

Dr. Angell,

Regarding young George, it was interesting to me how very aware he was, when he entered sixth grade at Merrill, of how well you had prepared him. He said so several times during the year! You made such an impression on so many young lives, and your pedagogy and professionalism was always top notch. Thank you for all you did for our child and so many others. His days in your classroom were the stuff that educators dream about: filled with discovery and passion for learning and encouragement to be his best self. We have so many fond memories of you and that precious education. Everything from the garden pesto to the dissections to the Montessori way of learning grammar. I think it is a rare thing for a teacher to make such an impact on one so young, but you did! We will forever be grateful.

Appendix A
Montessori's Model of Child Development: Four Planes

The organizing principle of Montessori's developmental theory is the idea that human growth does not proceed smoothly or steadily along a linear path toward self-improvement, but rather passes through a sequence of six-year stages she called planes of development. Each plane consists of two distinctive segments of three years—the first three years characterized by discovery and acquisition followed by three years during which the individual integrates and consolidates the learning gains of the first segment.

Montessori's model for the planes of development is a series of triangles descending from a horizontal line that represents the age progression from birth to twenty-four years. The descending lines on the left side of each triangle represent a period during which new knowledge is explored and new abilities are acquired. The ascending lines forming the right side of each triangle represent the three-year period when there is integration and consolidation of the new acquisitions. The turning points (where the descending line angles back toward the horizon) at ages three, nine, and fifteen years represent peaks of creative power. When a plane of development begins, the new direction takes the individual on a kind of detour that may appear to be disorganization but is actually the appearance of totally new interests and characteristics, a path to dramatically new kinds of learning.

Think of the infant from birth until three years. What tremendous new acquisitions there are in the movements and utterances, in the explorations and efforts of the baby orienting to the world. The discovery process includes chewing on blankets and fingers and spoons, flopping clumsily over to learn to roll at first and to crawl later, all kinds of sound experiments before recognizable language bits are spoken, and two-year-old attempts to master the art of getting dressed that can go on for hours. As this segment of the first plane comes to a close, at a peak of exploration and experimentation, the three-year-old child becomes ready for the Montessori primary class. There the child has the opportunity to integrate and consolidate all of the discoveries and experiences acquired during the first three years. Primary teachers watch these small children organize their sensory experiences into orderly progressions, learn to translate their spoken language into sentences and written words, and develop personal management skills making them remarkably independent individuals.

About the time of their sixth birthday, however, just as adults feel relieved that their offspring have begun to pick up their toys, fold their own laundry, and write tidy little notes, these children enter the second plane of development. They lose interest in tidiness, their questions change from what to why, and they begin taking intellectual risks of the imagination. The direction of their development has taken a downturn from the lifeline. They have entered back into that period of disorganization and discovery; they are ready for the Montessori elementary program. It is a place of great work, of passionate research and experimentation. The six- to nine-year-olds welcome every new experience without a need to tie things together or see a finished product. Lower elementary teachers take this opportunity to introduce key ideas in all of the academic disciplines and encourage the students to explore to the farthest reaches of their imagination. The classroom is a rollicking, busy, sometimes chaotic mix of discovery experiences and new acquisitions.

Then the creative power peaks, and the direction changes. The child is about nine years old when he or she begins to make connections between ideas, to care how finished products look and how they are received by others, to notice again how the order of things matter. This is the child ready to move into the completion of the second plane of development—into the upper elementary class, where integration and consolidation can take place.

Similar to the primary class, the three years of the upper elementary class capitalize on the discoveries and experiences of the first three elementary years. One might say these are the payoff years, the completion of a process begun with such fervor and energy in the lower elementary class. Children who complete six years of the elementary Montessori program have an opportunity to build on and synthesize all the explorations and experiences of their elementary career.

At age twelve the character and mood and direction of learning changes again as preadolescents enter the third plane of development. Again there is a period of disorientation, disorganization, discomfort, and discovery, this passage being well documented by middle school teachers as well as parents of new teens. It is a difficult time calling for a new environment to meet the needs of the emerging individual. For this very special person, there is a very special Montessori middle school program called Erdkinder, "children of the land."

Appendix B

John Dewey's Metaphor for Modern Schools: The Traveler with a Map

For the last two hundred years, two metaphors for education have prevailed. Students have been characterized either as empty vessels to be filled by the teacher or plants that will naturally unfold and flower without much intervention. In the first, the teacher is the active agent or responsible party who inscribes the empty slate (the brain) with learning. In the second case, it is up to the child to grow into an educated person with little intervention by the teacher, except for regular watering. The first is a transmission model, the second a kind of laissez-faire schooling.

In a 1902 essay entitled "The Child and the Curriculum," John Dewey explored the two metaphors—the transmission of the established school curriculum and the unfolding child. He found both inadequate for conceptualizing the process of educating youth. He asserted that true education is the passage between the developing intellect and the cultural intelligence the school is designed to transmit. His metaphor for this process is a learner on a journey with the aid of a map, a process aimed at self-construction.

Dewey's metaphor is consistent with the pedagogical theory of Maria Montessori. The Montessori classroom provides a learning environment that invites every individual to engage with the curriculum by freely choosing activities. We call this process self-direction. The environment provides the map, but every child must take their own unique trip.

Appendix C

Montessori Math Materials for the Elementary Classroom

1. A box of wooden stamps—green squares marked 1, blue squares marked 10, red ones labeled 100, and green again marked 1,000. These stamps can be laid out on a table and manipulated to demonstrate carrying, borrowing, multiplying, and distributive division. The work has many levels and is usually accompanied by squared paper for writing down problems and resulting answers. Emphasis is not on accuracy so much as process—and the counting to 10. The three colors for the hierarchies remain constant for many of the materials described below.

2. Three kinds of bead frames (abacuses) at increasing levels of difficulty—used for counting, learning place value, and computing.

3. Charts showing the facts of the four operations at several levels of abstraction, aids to memorization.

4. Boxes of bead bars representing the number sets

1–10, useful for games that help children conceptualize number sets, multiplication sets including squares, and beginning algebraic functions.

5. A rectangular checkerboard (about 30" by 12") laid out in colored squares with hierarchical value so that a bead bar might represent six or six hundred or six million, depending on its placement. This material is used primarily for multiplication.

6. Colored beads organized in racks and tubes (ten each) representing number hierarchies and a set of boards with indentations where the beads are distributed equally to calculate quotients. Often called test tube division, the material provides a tactile introduction to distributive division.

7. A set of metal frames holding circles divided into fractions, from halves to tenths, and an accompanying box of similar wedges for executing the operations with fractions.

8. A yellow board with longitudinal divisions for whole numbers and decimals accompanied by a box of beads and tiny cubes to represent decimal quantities. Again, the operations can be represented visually and sums or differences calculated with these materials.

9. A big square checkerboard used with bead bars for calculating decimal multiplication.

10. Large square peg boards with accompanying pegs in three colors to represent the hierarchies. These boards are used first to find multiples, later to inves-

tigate the divisibility of numbers, to build the squares of large numbers, and, finally, to represent and calculate square roots.

11. A large wall cabinet (the bead cabinet) housing bead chains as long as the square and cube of each number with small containers of tickets for labeling the chains. Also in this cabinet are the squares and cubes of each number 1–10 made of beads.

12. A large wooden box containing the number of wooden squares needed to build the cubes of each number 1–10 along with the solid wooden cubes, each number having its own distinctive color matching the colors of bead bars.

Appendix D
Geometry Materials for the Elementary Montessori Classroom

1. The geometry cabinet of plane figures, with six drawers of wooden figures together with its surrounding template, as follows: (a) three forms including the square, the circle, and the equilateral triangle; (b) six different kinds of triangles, not including the equilateral triangle; (c) six quadrilaterals; (d) six polygons, from pentagon to decagon; (e) six circles with dissimilar diameters; and (f) figures bounded by curved lines including the oval, the ellipse, and the curvilinear triangle.

2. The geometry nomenclature, a child's library of geometry figures with pictures, labels, and definitions in three parts: booklets with loose materials; accompanying booklets matching each folder; and wall charts, which show all the pictures with labels from a single chapter. A wall chart might show pictures of all the parts of a rectangle with the terms used for each

143

below the picture, a kind of advertisement for the nomenclature chapter that has been introduced or is being studied by a group of students.

3. Set of small solid wooden figures for holding and handling, including a sphere, an oval, an ellipse, a cone, a rectangular solid, a cube, and a cylinder.

4. Three boxes of constructive triangles, each one containing a different set of triangles assembled to show six different quadrilaterals and how they are formed. The third box in the set contains twelve identical triangles—the 3-4-5-right-angled triangle of Pythagoras with which one can construct amazing stars and variations.

5. A second set of three boxes of constructive triangles, each one containing a particular set of triangles used to demonstrate equivalencies among triangles, quadrilaterals and hexagons, culminating in proofs of the Pythagorean theorem.

6. A series of nine metal insets for work with similarity, equivalence, and congruence. One inset is a solid square. Four insets divide the square up into squares and rectangles resulting in halves, fourths, and eighths that are quadrilaterals, and another four are divided up into triangular halves, fourths, eighths, and sixteenths.

7. Insets of Equivalence. Metal insets designed for proofs that show the equivalence of figures such as a triangle and a rectangle with the same bases and altitudes.

Another pair of insets includes the decagon divided into triangles and an equivalent rectangle with an intermediate form to demonstrate the formula for calculating the area of polygons. The Insets of Equivalence contain three different insets for proving the Pythagorean theorem.

Appendix E
The Montessori Grammar Symbols

Instead of the traditional parts of speech, Montessori grammar is organized by the function of words, suggesting the jobs each group does to create the sense in language. A symbol is associated with each group as follows:

The noun names someone or something. The symbol is a black equilateral triangle to suggest how old the naming function is (think coal buried deep in the earth or the ancient pyramids).

The adjective describes a noun and so belongs to its family. The symbol is a dark blue equilateral triangle.

The article is another member of the noun family symbolized by a light blue triangle.

The verb expresses action, and its symbol is a bright red ball suggesting the energy of the sun and constant movement.

The adverb describes verbs, so its symbol is a smaller orange ball that hovers around the verb like a planet.

The pronoun is closely associated with the verb but can

also be used as a replacement for the noun. Therefore, it is part of the verb family, but the symbol is a purple isosceles triangle to suggest the prince who sometimes stands in for the king, the noun.

The preposition symbol is a small green quarter moon positioned like a bridge to suggest its function as a connector between words.

The conjunction also connects words or phrases, so the symbol is a small pink dash.

The interjection symbol takes the shape of a gold exclamation mark.

Notes

Chapter 1. August: The Mapmaker

1. Maria Montessori, *To Educate the Human Potential*, (Madras, India: Kalashektra, 1948/1973), p. 24.
2. Maria Montessori, *Dr. Montessori's Own Handbook*, (New York: Schocken, 1914/1965), pp. 136–138.

Chapter 2. September: The Storyteller

1. Maria Montessori, *To Educate the Human Potential*, (Madras, India: Kalashektra, 1948/1973), p. 15.
2. Maria Montessori, *To Educate the Human Potential*, (Madras, India: Kalashektra, 1948/1973), p. 27.
3. "The Galaxy Song/Lighten Up" is Jim Post's adaptation of Eric Idle's song "The Galaxy." Post recorded his rendition on the album *Crooner from Outer Space*, (Freckle Records, 1984).

Chapter 3. October: The Companion

1. Maria Montessori, *Dr. Montessori's Own Handbook*, (New York: Schocken, 1914/1965), pp. 132–33.
2. Maria Montessori, *Spontaneous Activity in Education: The Advanced Montessori Method Vol. I*, trans. Florence Simmonds and Lily Hutchinson (Adyar, Madras 20, India: Kalakshetra Publications, 1918/1965), p. 93.
3. Peter Menzel, *Material World: A Global Family Portrait*, (San Francisco: Sierra Club Books, 1995).

Chapter 4. November: The Community Organizer

1. Maria Montessori, *To Educate the Human Potential*, (Madras, India: Kalashektra, 1948/1973), p. 5.

Chapter 5. December: The Mirror

1. Howard Glasser and Tom Grove, *The Inner Wealth Initiative: The Nurtured Heart Approach*, (Tucson: Nurtured Heart Publications, 2007), pp. 70-71.

Chapter 6. January: The Psychologist

1. Maria Montessori, *Dr. Montessori's Own Handbook*, (New York: Schocken, 1914/1965), p. 133–134.

2. June Behrens, *Martin Luther King Jr.: The Story of a Dream*, (Children's Press: Holiday Play Books, 1979).

3. Lancelot Hogben, *The Wonderful World of Mathematics*, (New York: Garden City Books, 1955).

4. Virginia Lee Burton, *Life Story: The Story of Life on our Earth from its Beginning up to Now*, (New York, Houghton Mifflin Company, 1962, reprinted in China, 1990). Note: Although this book is out of print, it is worth hunting down for its graphic time lines, its presentation of evolution as a theatrical drama, and its detailed illustrations. On pages 43 and 45, I have always changed the word *man* to *human*—both as I read aloud and right on the page.

5. Angeline Stoll Lillard, *Montessori: The Science Behind the Genius*, (New York: Oxford University Press, 2005), p. 95.

6. Maria Montessori, *Spontaneous Activity in Education: The Advanced Montessori Method Vol. I*, trans. Florence Simmonds and Lily Hutchinson (Adyar, Madras 20, India: Kalakshetra Publications, 1918/1965), pp. 101–102.

Chapter 7. February: The Tour Guide

1. Maria Montessori, *From Childhood to Adolescence*, (New York: Shocken, 1948/1976), p. 10.

2. Susan L. Roth, transcriber and illustrator, *Leon's Story*, (Farrar, Straus and Giroux [BYR], 2000).

3. Richard E. Leakey, *Human Origins*, (New York: Lodestar Books, E. P. Dutton, 1982).

4. Maria Montessori, *The Child, Society and the World: Unpublished Speeches and Writings*, (Amsterdam: Montessori-Pierson Publishing, 2009), p. 47.

5. Khephra Burns, *Mansa Musa*, illustrators Leo and Diane Dillon, (New York: Harcourt Children's Books, 1990).

Chapter 8. March: The Advocate

1. Maria Montessori, *To Educate the Human Potential*, (Madras, India: Kalashektra, 1948/1973), p. 4.

Chapter 9. April: The Ringmaster

1. Paula Polk Lillard, *Montessori Today: A Comprehensive approach to Education from Birth to Adulthood*, (New York: Schocken, 1996), p. 50.

2. Ralph Waldo Emerson, *Essays: First Series*, (1841).

Chapter 10. May: The Student

1. Maria Montessori, *The Absorbent Mind*, trans. C. A. Claremont, (New York: Henry Holt, 1967a), pp. 75, 84.

2. Joseph Bruchac, *Pushing Up the Sky: Seven Native American Plays for Children*, (New York: Dial Books for Young Readers, 2000).

Chapter 11. June: The Reflective Practitioner

1. Maria Montessori, *The Child, Society, and the World: Unpublished Speeches and Writings (Vol. 7)*. Oxford: Clio, 1989, p. 28.

2. Maria Montessori, *Spontaneous Activity in Education: The Advanced Montessori Method Vol. I*, trans. Florence Simmonds and Lily Hutchinson, (Adyar, Madras 20, India: Kalakshetra Publications, 1918/1965).

Bibliography

Glasser, Howard and Tom Grove. *The Inner Wealth Initiative: the Nurtured Heart Approach.* Tucson: Nurtured Heart Publications, 2007.

Kohn, Alfie and Lois Bridges. *The Case Against Standardized Testing: Raising the Scores, Ruining the Schools.* New Hampshire: Heinemann, 2001.

Lillard, Angeline Stoll. *Montessori: the Science Behind the Genius.* New York: Oxford University Press, 2005.

Lillard, Paula Polk. *Montessori Today: A Comprehensive Approach to Education from Birth to Adulthood.* New York: Schocken, 1996.

Montessori, Maria. *The Montessori Method.* New York: Schocken, 1912/1964.

———. *Dr. Montessori's Own Handbook.* New York: Schocken, 1914/1965.

———. *The Advanced Montessori Method II* (A. Livingston, trans.) Oxford: Clio, 1916.

———. *Spontaneous Activity in Education: The Advanced Method* (Simmonds F., trans.) New York: Schocken, 1917/1965.

———. *The Secret of Childhood* (Carter, B. B., trans.) New York: Frederick A. Stokes, 1939.

——. *Education for a New World*. Madras, India: Kalakshetra, 1949/1963.

——. *To Educate the Human Potential*. Madras, India: Kalakshetra, 1948/1967.

——. *From Childhood to Adolescence*. New York: Shocken, 1948/1976.

——. *Childhood Education*. Chicago: Henry Regnery, 1949/1974.

——. *The Child in the Family* (Cirillo, N. R., trans.) New York: Avon, 1956.

——. *The Secret of Childhood* (Costello, M. J., trans.) New York: Ballantine, 1966.

——. *The Absorbent Mind* (Claremont, C. A., trans.) New York: Henry Holt, 1967a.

——. *The Discovery of the Child*. New York: Ballantine, 1967b.

——. *Education and Peace* (Lane, H.R., trans.) Washington, DC: Henry Regnery, 1972.

——. *Education for Human Development*. New York: Schocken, 1976.

——. *Child, Society, and the World: Unpublished Speeches and Writings (Vol. 7)*. Oxford: Clio, 1989.

——. *The California Lectures of Maria Montessori, 1915*. Oxford: Clio, 1997.

——. *The Child, Society, and the World: Unpublished Speeches and Writings*. Amsterdam: Montessori-Pierson Publishing, 2009.

CPSIA information can be obtained at www.ICGtesting.com
Printed in the USA
LVOW10s1055091014

407937LV00001B/1/P